DAVID SMITH
SCULPTURE AND WRITINGS BY
DAVID SMITH

Edited by Cleve Gray
With 148 illustrations, 7 in colour

Thames and Hudson

DAVID
SMITH
SCULPTURE AND WRITINGS
by DAVID
SMITH

Printed and bound in Singapore by C.S. Graphics

To Rebecca and Candida Smith

ACKNOWLEDGMENT

A few months after David Smith's death, the trustees of his estate turned over all his personal papers to the Archives of American Art. The Archives, with its regional headquarters in Detroit, was founded in 1954 for the purpose of finding, preserving and making available to scholars documents relating to American artists: personal notes, diaries, letters, sketches, drafts of essays and speeches, photographs. In the case of David Smith the collection is very rich. Covering the thirty-year period he worked as a sculptor, there are some 10,000 documents among which are several hundred photographs he made of his sculpture. It is almost exclusively from Archives material that I have edited this book.

As a result, I am deeply indebted to the Archives of American Art, to its President, W. E. Woolfenden, and especially to its Archivist, Garnett McCoy, whose assistance has been not only vital but sympathetic.

I thank the trustees of the Smith Estate—Ira Lowe, Clement Greenberg, and Robert Motherwell—for their permission to use this material. In particularly, I am deeply grateful for the consistent enthusiasm and kindness of Robert Motherwell.

David Smith's first wife, the sculptor Dorothy Dehner, was an invaluable help to me in checking facts in the autobiographical section; some of her comments concerning this period of their married life appear in the Appendix.

The suggestion for a book on David Smith first came to me from Jean Lipman, Editor-in-Chief of *Art in America*, after the completion of a feature on Smith which I edited in the January 1966 issue of that magazine. Mrs. Lipman and her husband, Howard, were devoted admirers of Smith's sculpture during his lifetime, and they gave me continual encouragement during the preparation of these pages.

Finally, I thank Alexander Liberman for his generous and wise advice.
C. G.

CONTENTS

FOREWORD

Few people who knew David Smith could forget him; his personality, like his frame, was powerful. He radiated energy, turbulence, and determination. He spoke and acted with decision. His positive and exuberant nature is reflected in his work. During the thirty years he labored as a sculptor he produced abundantly and heroically, and it is tragic that his death in May 1965 came at the time of his greatest achievements.

There are many artists, art critics, and collectors who already consider David Smith as the most important sculptor America has produced. Foremost among Smith's champions for the past 25 years has been Clement Greenberg; in 1943 Greenberg wrote that Smith was not only one of the best American sculptors but also that he had the potential to become the greatest. Today Greenberg sees not only the qualities of Smith's work but also "its unevenness, its sprawl, in all its bewildering diversity," and his judgment is that it "somehow remains open, unfinished."[1]

The lasting value of Smith's sculpture will be clarified by time, but his unique presence will be obscured. His booming voice, his hefty form, the red rage that could fill the air around him when his independence was challenged, his almost feminine tenderness with children, his appetites, his prejudices, all these faded when he died. Much of his human flavor is recaptured here, for his intimate thoughts are the content of this book. His moments of exhilaration, of depression, of inspiration, of slowly pondered ideas or hastily drawn sketches fill these pages with his presence. Side by side with the beautiful photographs he took of his own work, they are pages which form, to say the least, a unique document in the history of art.

"Oh David you are as delicate as Vivaldi, and as strong as a Mack truck."[2] These are words written by Smith's close friend, the painter Robert Motherwell. Poetic, graphic, and exact, they characterize the duality of Smith's nature, the conflict which he resolved in his sculpture. This kind of duality is symbolized by Smith's insistence that the best environment for his sculpture was outdoors. He loved the tensions at work when his machined forms, the gleaming aluminum, the painted steel thrust their manufactured shapes against sinuous nature in a classical Yin-Yang relationship. It was Motherwell who also wrote, "When I saw that David places his work against the mountains and sky, the impulse was plain, an ineffable desire to see his humanness related to exterior reality, to nature at least if not man, for the marvel of the felt scale that exists between a true work and the immovable world, the relation that makes both human."[3] David Smith did not like to see his sculpture indoors, constrained by architecture. Fighting constraints, his sculpture grew larger and larger. He had a sketch for an 18,000-foot "airscape," he wanted to build sculpture on a railroad flatcar, there were no limits to his dreams; and, in the same way, he wished to see these large forms without roofs and walls to hold them in.

He lived his life without constraints. When he was twenty years old he left his native Indiana and settled in New York City. A year later, in 1927, he married his first wife, Dorothy Dehner; together they bought, in the summer of 1929, a farm property in Bolton Landing, New York, overlooking Lake George. At first, he and his wife lived there only in

Photo by Irving Penn, 1964

Photo by Paul Rugile, 1935

Photo by A. Eriss, 1936

12

Photo by Dan Budnik, 1964

Photo by Alexander Liberman, May 1965

summertime; there was no heat, electricity, or plumbing, but gradually, as the city became too confining for his expansive spirit, with the few dollars they were able to spare, they built a home to live in and work in permanently.

Dorothy Dehner writes about their first full year in Bolton Landing: "We only moved into the house the year before I left, and we had only a wood stove to cook on, oil lamps, no plumbing . . . the water had to be pulled up out of the well . . . kindling chopped . . . etc. (all woman's work). I didn't mind in the least . . . being a city girl I thought it was fun. . . ."[4] This kind of pioneering life was close in Smith's past; it is said that his great-great-grandfather founded Decatur, Indiana; his grandfather used to delight him with stories about trouble with the Indians. The importance of this rough life to Smith was well understood by another friend, the critic Hilton Kramer, who wrote, "Smith's workshop in the mountains . . . brings together two old-fashioned ideas of American life: the proud individualism and keen workmanship of the man who lives on his own land. Both are ideals of freedom out of the American past, derived from the ethos of a harder but simpler life than most Americans find possible to live now, and they are supported in Smith's case by an unsentimental grasp of the difficulty involved in sustaining such freedom in a social environment where success no less than failure can deprive one of its realization. We might say that everything about Smith's work is up-to-date but the style of life which makes it possible for him to create it."[5]

Coupled with the toughness that made David Smith want to live in the mountains, that enabled him to have worked as a logger, an oiler, a welder in a locomotive factory, was a refined sensitivity that made him a gourmet, a man who could cook memorable dinners, serve great wines, who loved Bach, Renaissance furniture, and whose consuming passion was sculpture and painting.

One weekend, only a few days before he was killed, I took my family up to Lake George to see David and his new work. We were accompanied by the Robert Motherwells and by my in-laws, the Alexander Libermans. It was this weekend which I described in *Art in America*, January 1966. All of us were stunned by the pageantry of his sculpture, which he had ranged outside like an army of behemoths massed down the grassy slopes which opened out from the forests. Though he enjoyed our gaping enthusiasm at what he called his sculpture farm, his first anxiety was for the comfort of his guests. He found two tricycles for my four- and five-year-old sons to ride on, he scurried for drinks to give us, he bustled over the elaborate lunch he himself was cooking. His own pleasure with our visit was captivating; it was revealed by many sensitive touches: iced fruit in a crystal bowl, Bordeaux, *blanc de blancs* and Champagne, fresh filet of sole—a rarity in the Adirondacks—meats that he had smoked himself, asparagus steamed in a Chinese manner, mounds of cheese. He was as excited about his cooking as a professional chef might be, disappointed when it wasn't as perfect as he wanted it and naïvely pleased with success. He would embrace us like a bear and repeat, "You don't know how happy I am that you are all here!" One sensed how lonely he was without his family.

He was the cause of his own loneliness, without doubt. His second marriage, begun so hopefully and fulfilled so happily with two daughters, Rebecca and Candida, ended in a bitter divorce. A source of this unhappiness must certainly have been the authoritarian and destructive side to his nature that made him a difficult partner. Many of David's relationships ended in conflict. He crusaded violently for his ideas, he took offense easily, he was uncompromising, suspicious, and like every artist, egotistical. He was determined to assert the freedom his spirit needed; a freedom he believed an artist was entitled to. But he often argued with the very people who were helping him because of his ferocious indignation over a misunderstanding. When Emily Genauer first met him before World War II, she called him "an angry young man bursting with bitterness about the state of the world."[6] At that time Smith had just finished his series of antiwar medals, "Medals for Dishonor," exhibited at the Willard Gallery accompanied by his own prose poems which passionately revealed his outraged feelings. Though in later years his political ideas mellowed into a calmer liberalism, he never lost his quick fury over injustices, personal or impersonal, imagined or real. He lashed out to defend himself, but no artist fought more consistently than he to improve the lot of deserving art students or professionals. As a result, it was natural that President Johnson appointed him to the National Council on the Arts. He was proud of this appointment; he kept the President's letter tacked to his kitchen door along with photographs of and notes from his daughters, reproductions of art he admired, menus he had enjoyed. On the weekend we spent with him, his mind was full of plans to present to the National Council at the next meeting in Washington.

David Smith's own words are the clearest revelation of his ideas. The major part of this book is devoted to those words. As he matured, he slowly formulated his thoughts; he rewrote, again and again, speeches or statements he made at universities or museums: brief notes, sentences, and paragraphs were accumulated over extended periods. He seems to have kept every paper he possessed, and, fortunately for his biographers, these papers have been preserved by the Archives of American Art. Some of them are reproduced here in facsimile. David's handwriting was clear, bold, generous, unpretentious, masculine, large, energetic, and consistent. Looking at it one sees no smallness, nothing cramped, erratic, flaccid, affected, or fanciful. He formed his letters and his thoughts with the same deliberation. Among the 10,000 Smith documents in the Archives of American Art I drew from for this book, some of the most remarkable are his poems. His poetry and often his prose have a Whitmanesque power which, like the quality of his photographs, is unexpected. A long chapter is devoted to his notebooks, drawings, and paintings. He was not an important painter, but these pages reveal many of the incipient stages of his sculptural ideas. He drew them from the most varied sources: canopic jars, natural history museum skeletons or stuffed animals, country landscapes and city perspectives, nudes, newspaper photographs, Near Eastern seals, hieroglyphs, machinery, medical book illustrations, newspaper horror stories, classic philosophy, Chinese communism.

Almost all of Smith's friends were artists, and most of these were painters. Naturally he gravitated to collectors and critics who admired his work, but his deepest friendships were with artists—the painters Robert Motherwell, Helen Frankenthaler, Kenneth Noland, Herman Cherry, and the sculptor James Rosati. An exception was his first art dealer, Marian Willard, and her husband, Daniel Johnson. Their association and friendship lasted many years; it was rare for Smith to maintain a harmonious relationship with business associates. No doubt each of David's friends would describe him differently. Marian Willard, speaking of his relentless creative drive, says, "This enormous energy remains in my mind as his predominant characteristic."[7] Herman Cherry has written, "David was a man who could be Mr. Hicksville in Bolton Landing and a sophisticate in a New York drawing room. Or reverse the roles if his humor dictated it. This sometimes confused his admirers and helped create the myths circulating during his lifetime. He was a thoroughly sophisticated man and well aware of the picture he was creating. He had a Yankee shrewdness, especially about money . . . David had many secret lives. Even his closest friends had no idea of the different worlds he moved in. His trips to New York were an amalgam of business and deep interest in keeping up with the art world. He had an insatiable compulsion to work. It reached moral proportions. Even on these trips he would make some drawings. He loved to brag about the numbers of drawings he made a year—over 300. He would set goals for himself that seemed superhuman, and although a sensual man with vast appetites, he held to the rigors of a monastic life in his work. This dichotomy plagued him all his life."[8]

Those friends of David who were present at his funeral on the shore of Lake George will not easily forget the words of James Rosati. Recounting what David was like, Rosati said that the one characteristic that seemed best to describe him was "luxuriousness." This pervaded both his actions and his concepts of art. Rosati told how one day he had gone with David to buy some drawing paper; they both had very little money, and Rosati was careful to buy only a few sheets. Smith began to order ream upon ream of the handmade paper, and Rosati was aghast, knowing Smith couldn't afford such quantities. He finally turned to Smith and said, "Gee, it must be wonderful to afford paper like that!" to which David replied, "Hell, man, who can afford it? Making art is a luxury."[9]

Kenneth Noland was David's youngest close friend. Knowing this I asked Noland to write a few words about David for *Art in America*'s memorial feature. Noland let many weeks pass before he sent me his answer. Finally he told me that he had thought a lot about what he could say and that it was the way David worked that seemed most important. "David knew more about how to go about working than any other artist I've known personally; in this sense he was an example for us all."[10]

But, in the end, is it how others see an artist that counts or rather how he sees himself? The recurring theme that runs through David Smith's thoughts, as they are revealed in his writing, is the importance of self-recognition, of asserting his own identity. "The truly creative substance in the work of art is the artist's identity." "Our own truth as the artist is our dominant identity." "The sculpture work is a statement of my own identity." "The identity does not yield." "It is identity, and not that overrated quality called ability, which describes the artist's finished work." "Beneath the whole art concept, every pass in the act, every stroke should be our own identity. . . ." This is the base motif of Smith's convictions; it re-echoed through his concepts of art and determined his life. He hammered at this conviction as hard as he hammered at iron on an anvil, he tried to shape his life according to it.

The struggle to realize his own identity was the source of the art that David Smith has left us. But what this achievement meant in terms of his suffering is something we must guess at. It is a guess, though, educated by one of the most moving revelations of an artist's loneliness ever written, the pages in the text which begin "And so this being the happiest—is disappointing . . ." and which end with the cry, "I hate to go to bed—to stay alive longer—I've slipped up on time—it all didn't get in—the warpage is in me—I convey it to the person I live with—where do I find it to charge—do I like it that way, am I glad it's too late—some yes some no—would financial security help—or why cannot part security till May be some appeasement." How strange his mention of May, for it was on a May evening that, driving alone, he missed a curve in the road and was crushed inside his truck.

CLEVE GRAY

DAVID SMITH
by
DAVID SMITH

The works you see are segments of my
work life. If you prefer one work over
another, it is your privilege, but it does not
interest me. The work is a statement
of identity, it comes from a stream,
it is related to my past works, the
3 or 4 works in process and the work
yet to come. I will accept your
rejection but I will not consider your
criticism any more than I will concerning
my life.

Group: *Swung Forms*, steel, 1937; *Chain Head*, steel, 1933;
Agricola Head, steel, 1933

Group: (above) *Reclining Figure*, steel, 1935;
(below) *Landscape*, cast iron/steel, 1935

Head as Still Life,
bronze/cast iron/steel, 1936

Leda, steel, 1938

EVENTS IN A LIFE

Of course I get rides on when I'm working. I get so wound up
at my work I can't get sleepy and work through 3 4 5 or daylight.
Did this back in Brooklyn. All my life the workday has been any
any part of the 24—on oil tankers, driving hack, going to school,
all three shifts in factories. I'd hate to live a routine life.
Any 2/3 of the whole 24 are wonderful as long as I choose.

Interior for Exterior, steel/bronze, 1939

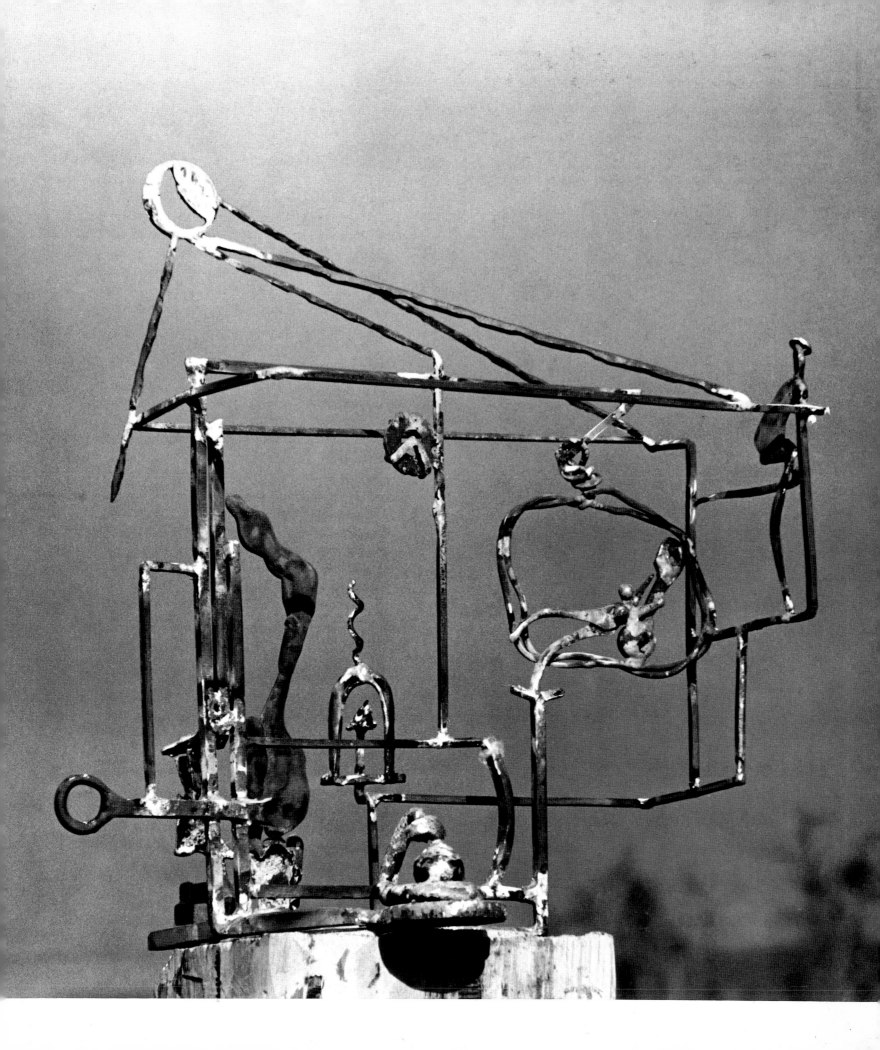

Editor's note: Some time around 1950, David Smith composed the brief autobiography, covering his life until 1947, printed below. It was found in his files after his death. The integrity of Smith's style has been retained in this transcript, as it has been throughout the entire volume; only minor spelling or typist's mistakes have been altered. Smith's comments in the autobiography, the events he chose to include or omit, his errors in dates or facts are all part of this absorbing and important document. Numbered notes mark some obvious editorial explanations and added comments by his first wife, Dorothy Dehner, which are made under Notes to the Text in the Appendix.

1906   Born—Decatur, Indiana March 9, 1906.

Grade school and high school at Decatur

Moved to Paulding, Ohio in 2nd year of high school.

Went to Ohio University 1924 (studying art).

1925   Worked in South Bend summer of 1925

Studebaker factory—riveter on frame assembly worked on lathe—soldering jig—spot welder. Did it strictly for money—more than I ever made in my life.

Worked for Banking Agency of Studebaker finance department and was transferred to Morris Plan bank at Washington D. C. Studied poetry for one semester at George Washington University because they had no art courses. Always been interested in poetry.

1926   Fall of 1926 transferred to New York bank of Morris Plan bank (called Industrial Acceptance Corp.)

Studied at Art Students' League—studied with Richard Lahey—academic painter, now director of Corcoran Art School.

1927   Early summer of 1927 transferred back to South Bend office and then fired at end of summer.

Drove back to New York with two friends:

    Jerry Strauss—Paris (connected with same Co.)

    Blanchard—Studebaker dealer in Switzerland

Went to Art Students' League—studied painting with John Sloan from Sloan—got a certain amount of feeling—of knowing the artist's position as a rebel or as one in revolt against status quo—heard about cones and cubes and Cézanne from him.

Studied woodcut with Allen Lewis

Married Dorothy Dehner, December 23, 1927[1] painter.

Shifted around to study with KIMON NICHOLADIES drawing "feeling for sensitivity in a line" drove a taxi from 4:00 A. M. till noon to earn living[2]

1928   Free lance art work. Then in early Spring of 1928 shipped out of Philadelphia on an oil tanker for San Pedro, thru Panama. Stayed for summer—returned on oil tanker to Bayonne, N.J. Free lance art work.[3]

Got job at A. G. Spalding and Bros.[4] sports goods house—window display etc. Kept up studies at Art Students' League—studied with Jan Matulka—painter (student of Hans Hofmann).

"Great Awakening of Cubism" Matulka was the kind of a teacher that would say—"you got to make abstract art"—got to hear music of Stravinsky—Have you read the "Red and the Black"—"Stendhal" Language was not fluent but he was right for me at that time. Matulka was a guy I'd rather give more credit than anyone else.[5]

1930   Was offered a job in an advertising agency. N. W. Ayer and Sons (working some nights as art Editor for a magazine called "Tennis" official publisher of USLTA (US Lawn Tennis Ass'n).

1932   Fall of 1932 went to Virgin Islands[6] and painted—returned to New York in June.

Trip was probably motivated by Romanticism of Gauguin.

While in Virgin Islands—painted (color photos exist) In the Virgin Islands I painted very seriously and very well—Large and small paintings—made sculpture[7] (stone sculpture) out of chunks of sculpture started my first interest in fish bones and broken shells etc.—Spent some time taking photos.

'33 Spring of 1933 went up to Bolton Landing N. Y. and continued making sculpture in wood—wire—melted lead and painted Constructions wood wire stone aluminium rod, (photos) coral I had brought back. Sculpture grew out of my work with MATULKA in the study of textures, moths etc.—was a very live guy—introduced us to Kandinsky, De Stijl, Cubism, etc.

(Still enjoy painting—paint 2 or 300 brush drawings a year).

Fall of 1933 made up some things and took them to Barney Snyder's garage—a garage in Bolton and welded them together. First iron sculptures I made (prompted by seeing the work of Picasso which I have been told were created jointly with Gonzalez (See 1932 Cahier d'Art)[8] Constructed sculptures

Make definite outright thanks to cubism and constructivism.[9]

    Gargallo—(earliest iron working in Spanish)

    Gonzalez—(tradition)

When I saw the liberation made by Picasso in the work, I was told Gonzalez had helped him.

Since I had worked in factories and made parts of automobiles and had worked on telephone lines I saw a chance to make sculpture in a tradition I was already rooted in.

In fall of 1933—went back to New York and got a job again at Spalding's—bought a welding outfit (same one I have now) air reduction oxy-acetelyne welding torch—lived in apartment 124 State Street.

Fall of 1933 knew artists who were all friends and companions Edgar Levy—Lucille Corcoa, Adolph Gottlieb, Lew Harris, Lew Shanker, and others—Gregorio Prestopino.

Started working in the back room with my new welding outfit. Things were catching fire[10]—Landlord worried about noise and fire. One Sunday afternoon we were walking on navy pier. Down below on the ferry terminal was a long rambly junky looking shack called Terminal Iron Works. Wife said, "David that's where you ought to be for your work." Next morning I walked in and was met by a big Irishman named Blackburn. "I'm an artist, I have a welding outfit. I'd like to work here." "Hell! yes—move in." With Blackburn and Buckhorn I moved in and started making sculpture there.[11] I learned a lot from those guys and from the machinist that worked for them named Robert Henry. Played chess with him, learned a lot about lathe work from him.

Between Terminal Iron Works at 1 Atlantic Ave. and George Kiernan's Saloon at 13 Atlantic Ave., I met about everyone on the water front in our area—Many who were very good friends provided me with metal—Kind of a nice "fraternity" down there. Enjoyed this.

Those guys were fine—never made fun of my work—took it as a matter of course.

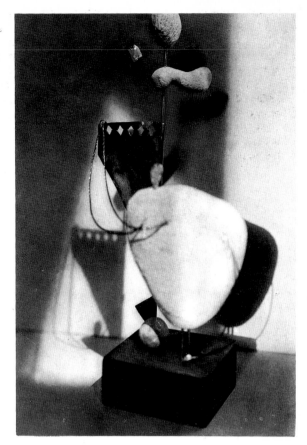

Construction, wire/wood/stone, 1932–33

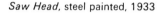

Saw Head, steel painted, 1933

Terminal Iron Works, Brooklyn, c. 1934

In the case of Blackburn and Buckhorn—there were times when I couldn't pay my rent[12]—I'd go out on a ship and work with them for a few days and we'd call the rent even.

Exhibited my first paintings at the ACA Gallery[13] when it was located uptown and was essentially a frame shop.

Showed several blue print water color drawings at Ferargil galleries[14] same year (abstract paintings)

Moscow, photographed by Smith in 1935

1934 I showed two of my iron sculptures at Julien Levy Galleries along with several wood sculptures (big iron head).

Levy asked—"This head is not stuck together with chewing gum, is it?"

These were the depression years—life was hard—taught for a short time at a Jewish Settlement house—(paid) worked thru a very good friend John Graham, who collected African sculpture for Frank Crowninshield; I was mounting (made bases) and helped in cataloguing.

Still making sculpture at Terminal Iron Works all this time.

Got on Public Works Art Project—

Paralleled P. W. A. P. (T. E. R. A.)? Supervising the technical procedures on murals.

Encouragement I got was primarily from the faith and encouragement I got from my wife Dorothy in these formative years.[15]

1935 A very good friend John Xceron had a show at Garland gallery. After the opening we were walking down the street for coffee. He persuaded me to give up painting and concentrate entirely on sculpture—but I didn't do this right away. I was already preparing to go to

Europe on a small inheritance from my Grandmother.[16]

Fall of 1935 went to Paris—(one month in Paris did some etchings in Hayter's studio—mixed media technique, drawing objective figures but picking up technique) went to Greece—had a studio in Athens at 26 Joseph Monferatu—Traveled over Greece—Studied at American School of Archeology—Did two sculptures which I had cast in bronze and abandoned them because of poor casting.[17] We came back on a boat to Naples, then to Malta (enjoyed seeing Neolithic Hypogeum there) Marseilles, then to Paris again. Went to London—early May—went to Sadler Wells Ballet and heard Thorez, French Communist, address (couldn't understand it) an open meeting in Hyde Park—Seeing sculpture British Museum from Greece—Egypt—Took a Russian Steamer to Leningrad and Moscow on a 21 day tour.

Saw Matisse—early Cézanne—Picasso etc. at Museum of Western Art. (When in Paris, my friend John Graham was there buying sculpture for Crowninshield. I looked up Graham's wife and children in Moscow. She was in charge of restoration in the Byzantine Museum)

Came back to New York in July 1936.

16   Bolton Landing in July—worked on sculpture in 1936—made "Reclining Figure" in converted wood shed at Bolton Landing. Welding equipment, no electricity—taking the day's work down to Bradley's riding stable—doing grinding and power equipment work—in his blacksmith shop. Late fall, back to New York and Terminal Iron Works.

17   (Pierre Matisse) took some photos and the "Reclining Figure" to Matisse gallery—Matisse said, "It looked better before you unwrapped it." Back to Terminal Iron.[18]

(Who were associated and who encouraged me in New York 1933 etc.? Stuart Davis—John Graham—Bill de Kooning—Mischa Resnikoff—Gorky)[19]

I remember very strongly the Spanish War in 1937 (Franco et al). I was a member of the artists union then (C. I. O. group). I remember an art auction in Brooklyn Heights for the benefit of the Spanish people—a lot of things were auctioned off—brought fair prices for that time. Since my work was abstract and came at the tail end of the auction it only brought $15.00[20] for a small figure (no photo of this piece) all happened too quick I didn't have time to protest—thought—Hell! I didn't have $15.00 to give to loyalists in Spain so if it goes it's ok in this case.

Bombing of Guernica didn't surprise me too much. I thought it was pretty much Capitalist Perfidity[21]—especially the way the blockade went—I had gone to Europe in 1935 to see it before I expected it to be bombed out of existence having read R. Palme Dutt (English writer but Indian—had written an analysis of Fascism. A Communist.) I was very saddened at the fall of Spain but I had also witnessed the invasion of Ethiopia by Fascism and was fully aware of the Nazi penetration of Greece when I was there.[22]

Produced quite a few works in 1937—Back at Terminal Iron Works

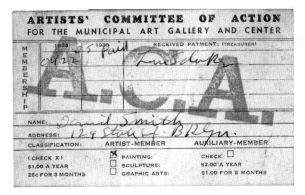

Membership as painter in ACA, 1935

Workshed, Bolton Landing, c. 1935

Construction in Bent Planes, steel, 1936

27

again. Working for the Treasury Department—surveying post offices for murals and mural installation.

Hananiah Harari,[23] who had seen my 1937 work at Leo Lance's while it was being photographed, recommended me to the East River gallery which was owned by Marian Willard and that winter (November or December) she came to my studio (57 Poplar—Brooklyn Heights) and agreed to give me an exhibition (1st one man show) which took place in 1938.

Practically all the sculpture in that show was iron with encaustic color. Didn't seem to arouse very much critical opinion.[24] Martha Davidson in Art News did a review.

1938 Kept working at Terminal Iron Works. Spent summer of 1938 at Bolton Landing. Continued my work on sculpture. Summer did a group of "lost wax" bronzes—Modelling and investing myself by having bronze poured in a machine foundry in Glens Falls, N. Y. Edward Alden Jewell made a remark about one of Smith's sculptures—I can see no earthly reason for its existence—in New York Times.[25]

1939 In the spring I had a show at Willard-J. B. Neumann[26] (Willard had her gallery with J. B. Neumann) Big fabrications of steel fixed in porcelain enamel—large piece[27]—exhibited at N. Y. World's Fair Exhibition. One of these exhibited at New York World's Fair 1940 (?) First piece I ever sold to a collector was out of this exhibition sold to George L. K. Morris—as I recall this was the only piece sold in the exhibition. I remember J. B. Neumann talking to Morris about it—

Head, cast iron/steel, 1938

His enthusiasm for my work etc. Lots of dealers come to my shows Contrary to what some artists and the general public feel that dealers exploit the artist—So far I don't think I've ever paid a dealer for his investment to 1940. One thing I remember about the Willard-Neumann show[28] was a wonderful write up by Elizabeth McCausland (writer of Sunday Art page for Springfield [Mass.] "Republican"). Clement Greenberg in "The Nation"[29] gave me a particularly complimentary review. "If Smith continues, promises to be first American sculptor" etc.

Sometime after this exhibition, thru Maria Martins (sculptor Maria, wife of Brazilian Ambassador) unbeknown to me at the time was influential in getting the money which was given to the Modern Museum for the purchase of "The Head". Only thing they have in their collection.[30]

Had an exhibition at Willard gallery[31] at 32 East 57th street on same floor with Curt Valentin BUCHHOLZ gallery.

From 1936 after I came back from Europe I was impressed by Sumerian Seals—Intaglio concept in general—a collection of war medals I had seen in British Museum.[32] I decided to do a series of Anti-war medallions called "Medals for Dishonor."

Worked at Terminal Iron Works by day and living on Congress street (near iron works) in Brooklyn Heights area. For three or four years I'd been working nights on this series of Medallions.[33] I was trying to cast them at iron works out of block tin—I abandoned all of the first year's work on these medals due to unsatisfactory [casting]. Did a new series—which I <u>had</u> cast in bronze.

Finally I wound up by finding a jeweler to cast them for me.

I remember talking to my dealer[34] and discussing the possibility of showing these at another gallery due to their nature. My dealer who has always been interested in my general welfare said ok go ahead. Went to ACA, Associated American and other galleries.

Everyone liked them but no one wanted to show them. Finally had a show of these at Willard Gallery in late '41.[35] War spirit had gained momentum to such an extent that it was a poor time to show them. Almost not quite ethical.

Since these were on a plane which I considered to be more classical in nature and Humanitarian in content and opposed to Fascist war ideology I still wanted to show them. I wanted a foreword written to this catalogue and after interviewing a number of people finally settled on William Blake—English writer (wrote) Showed him the work—Left some of the Medallions with him.

He and his wife (Christina Stead) Australian writer—"The Man Who Loved Children"—had been very enthusiastic about them so she as well as Blake had written a foreword so catalogue has two forewords. (See catalogue for text etc.)

I remember a very complimentary review by Milton Brown in PARNASSUS (1941?) Full page in Time—(Mr. Smith Comes to Town.)

On the Medallions.

Munition Maker—cast in silver and purchased from me by Marian Willard.

Medal for Dishonor: Bombing Civilian Populations, bronze cast, 1939

For PROPAGANDA FOR WAR

the rape of the mind by machines
of death — atop the curly bull
the red cross nurse blows
the clarinet — the elephant
flys — the stage is set
the web is spun. it is not the
fish story of Jonah but of
the chorus girl helping by
what she is most able

the speakers goad the mind and
offer red apples while the
radio parts the ether with
shrieks and emotional bombings.
the corny trumpet leaves
behind sour footnotes — the
walking speaker spews ballast
behind the nurse hang heavy
laden wires with atrocity
stories — of burned nuns —
dog eats child — death sells
hoover apples — torn bodies
and spilt milk.

the horse is dead in this hellfight
arena — the bull is docile can be ridden —

who caught the fish to which they fed
babies — the female auxiliary draws
attention to it.

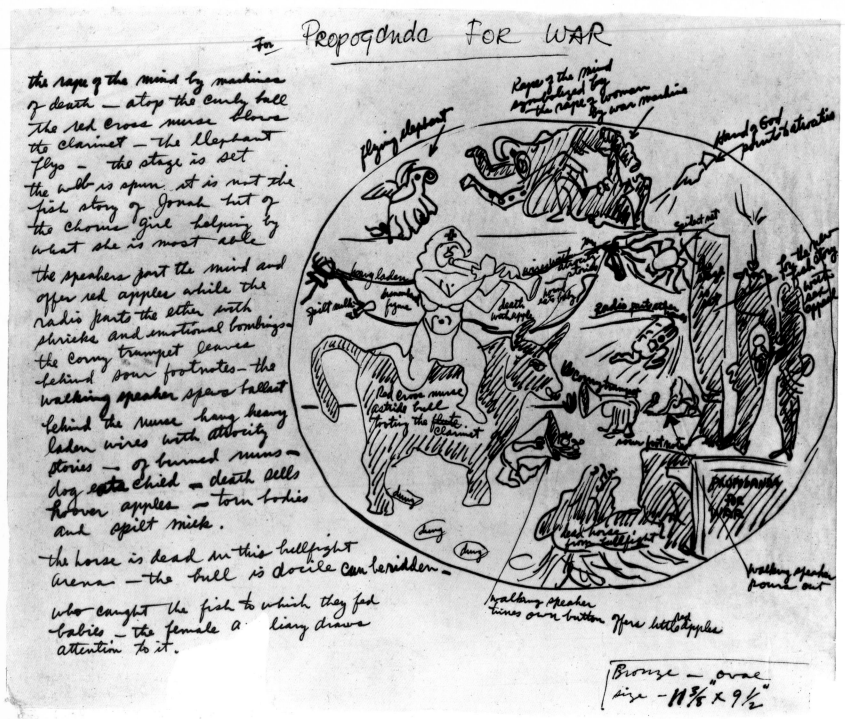

Medal for Dishonor: Propaganda for War, ink, 1939–40

Whether it's true or not, it seems to me that I've sold more work to critics and other artists[36] than I have to collectors and museums. I've never tabulated it but certainly I view with affection the fact that artists and critics have bought my work because it is true that an artist not only works for himself but he works for some audience, I would rather have the approval of other artists and critics than monetary sales reward. Maybe this is a rationalization but since it seems that that's about all I have, I naturally like it best. (Probably relates to my belligerence against collectors: rich people, museum people etc.)

1941   Had a show (of the Medals) at Willard—enthusiastically received—never sold a one. Very few of these medals owned. I had hoped to make 10 copies of each one. Several years later Joseph HIRSCHORN (New York collector) bought 3. JAN DE GRAAFF bought 1 (horticulturalist from Gresham, Oregon). Brooklyn pediatrician[37] who was a friend of Edgar Levy bought 1 (get name). Gave 1 to Christina and Bill Blake and traded 1 to Eliot Elisofon (check spelling with Millman; on Life mag staff)[38] for doing photographs.

1942   In 1940 I had been successful in making the electric co. give me light service to Bolton Landing house. Thru REA forced them to bring elect. service into our area and since their fee [was high] for bringing the line into the house which was 600' off the road—I built a studio down on the road—cut my own poles and strung my own wire. Designed and made this studio (on an industrial factory type) Was in debt for the building—new ice box, car and a truck.
Figured I better get a job—so I went down to Schenectady to employment office—hired in as a welder—got stuck with the graveyard shift. This new studio I had built, I had christened the Terminal Iron Works—partly because the change in my particular type of sculpture required a factory more than an "Atelier." Partly because I had already established credit thru the Terminal Iron Works in Brooklyn and because I had become the Terminal Iron Works after Buckhorn had sold out the equipment and gone to work for a government agency.
The last year I was in Brooklyn, until spring of 1940 when I moved up to Bolton, I was the Terminal Iron Works—Buckhorn's father was the Terminal Bone and Pearl Works since he had also sold his name with his business in Lower Manhattan. Buckhorn senior had made ivory, bone, pearl objects of every nature. He was a craftsman of the old school—at present time he was making revolver handles and caviar plates[39]—out of Australian pearl shell.
We got along well—made tea together on coals of a pot-bellied stove—I worked at Locomotive plant—we lived in an attic on McClelland Street in Schenectady. Went up to Bolton Landing every weekend we could.
During the war, I managed to make a few pieces of iron sculpture and finish some bronze sculpture[40] and when I was thru work at the factory at 8:00 A. M.—I would drive 2 or 3 days a week, 40 miles to Saratoga to the monument works of Mallory and LaBrake where I carved marble for 6 hours. Drove back to Schenectady and got

to bed—got up at 11:30 for midnight shift. These were hard and dull days for Dorothy and took a lot of faith and a lot of dependence entirely for the future;[41] about once a week I would get my sleep over in the day and we would drive to Saratoga for a night session—get a model to pose in a friend's studio—Just to keep drawing and to maintain my identity as an artist. Learned much about polishing and cutting from Papa Buckhorn. He had the front end of shop and I had the rear where the old forging beds were—we both worked quietly and seriously and productively. When I went to Schenectady I found it very difficult to make art when physical labor was so strenuous—many of the days were 12 hours and oftimes were involved with rush orders for narrow gauge steam engines for Africa and rush orders of tank destroyers for the same place.

I had been rejected by the army on sinus trouble[42] and the only consolation of the 7 days a week and the 12 hour days was the tools and equipment that the money would buy for my own sculpture making as soon as this was over.

While I was in the factory—I was rated by army ordnance as a 1st class armor plate welder. Also was recommended to the Chinese government as an artist to design medals for the Chinese army and at the request of T. V. SOONG'S division "China Defense Supplies" I had submitted some drawings and was chosen to do the commissions.

By this time I had been transferred to the cylinder shop in the locomotive works and was on the swing shift. A number of times I had gone to Washington D. C. in the morning for conferences and was back in the locomotive works, welding the main steam line, without missing more than 2 hours of my shift.

Stayed at this job until after V J day when the factory went on a 5 day week. I left on a lay off and didn't go back.

1944   Immediately I started making sculpture. Worked on my studio—finished work and finished the floor—together Dorothy and I designed a house which we decided to build.[43] I was able to sell enough timber off the place to pay for the house, and with our savings I bought the materials and stacked them in the field to make a block-type functional steel and cinder block house.

1945   Had worked diligently on sculpture and in summer of 1945 I was living and working alone because Dorothy had moved to N. Y.[44]

1946   Had so much work that it couldn't show at Willard Gallery alone, so my dealer (Marian Willard) arranged a joint show with Curt Valentin of Buchholz gallery.

This was a retrospective—most of early work in Willard gallery and recent work in Buchholz gallery. Dr. Wm. Valentiner did the foreword. Good acceptance—good sales. (who bought what?)

Whitney museum bought . . . "Cockfight Variation" made from drawing.

City Art museum of St. Louis . . . "Cockfight." It so happened that I had a small drawing in my book on "Cockfight." One day I picked up a piece of metal that had been cut from another sculpture. Its

The new house with Dorothy Dehner, Bolton Landing, c. 1944

grace and rhythm suggested my drawing. I don't go to cockfights but fighting roosters are raised by my friends in the hills and meets are regularly held near Saratoga.

I found the metal piece suggested the tail feathers of a fighting cock so I proceeded to make the rest of the rooster in relation to the piece of metal. Also the rooster with which it was fighting. When it was finished I found it in no way was related to the cubic structure which my drawing orginally had. So still having an interest in the subject as I had conceived it, I went ahead and did another cockfight based on the drawing and called #2 "Cockfight Variation."

Dealer Henry Kleeman bought a sculpture "The Ancient Household." Note—the year before (1945) the writer Victor Wolfson had bought a sculpture from Curt Valentin ("Woman Music").

In this year I made "Jurassic Bird"—etc. (see catalogue).

Show of the work I had done in 1946.[45]

Cockfight, ink, before 1945

Woman Music,
steel, 1945

Cockfight Variation,
steel, 1945

...fight,
1945

33

When I lived and studied in Ohio, I had a very vague sense of what art was. Everyone I knew who used that reverent word was almost as unsure and insecure.

Mostly art was reproductions, from far away from an age past and from some garden shore, certainly from no place like the mud banks of the Auglaze or the Maumee, and there didn't seem much chance that it could come from Paulding County.

Genuine oil painting was some highly cultivated act, that came like the silver spoon, born from years of slow method, applied drawing, water coloring, designing, art structure, requiring special equipment of an almost secret nature, that could only be found in Paris or possibly New York.

And when I got to New York and Paris I found that painting was made with anything at hand, building board, raw canvas, self-primed canvas with or without brushes, on the easel, on the floor, on the wall, no rules, no secret equipment no anything, except the conviction of the artist, his challenge to the world and his own identity.

Discarding the old methods and equipment will not of course make art. It has only been a symbol in creative freedom, from the bondage of tradition, and outside authority.

Sculpture was even farther away. Modeling clay was a mystic mess which came from afar. How a sculpture got into metal was so complex that it could only be done in Paris. The person who made sculpture was someone else an ethereal poetic character divinely sent, who was scholar, aesthetician, philosopher, continental gentleman so sensitive he could unlock the crying vision from a log, or a Galatea from a piece of imported marble.

I now know that sculpture is made from rough externals by rough characters or men who have passed through all polish and are back to the rough again.

The mystic modeling clay is only Ohio mud, the tools are at hand in garages and factories. Casting can be achieved in almost every town. Visions are from the imaginative mind, sculpture can come from the found discards in nature, from sticks and stones and parts and pieces, assembled or monolithic, solid form, open form, lines of form, or like a painting the illusion of form and sculpture can be painting and painting can be sculpture and no authority can overrule the artist in his declaration. Not even the philosopher, the aesthetician or the connoisseur.

Atmosphere of Early Thirties

One did not feel disowned—only ignored and much alone, with a vague pressure from authority that art couldn't be made here—it was a time for temporary expatriots, not that they made art more in France, but that they talked it—and when here were happier there—and not that their concept was more *avante* than ours but they were under its shadow there and we were in the windy openness here. Ideas were sought as the end but the result often registered in purely performance. Being far away, depending upon Cahier d'Art and the return of patriots often left us trying for the details instead of the whole. I remember watching a painter Gorky working over an area edge probably a hundred times to search an infinite without changing the rest of the picture, based upon Graham's recount of the import in Paris on the "edge of paint." We all grasped upon everything new, and despite the atmosphere of New York worked on everything but our own identities. I make exceptions for Graham and Davis—especially Davis who, though at his least recognized or exhibited stage, was the solid citizen for a group of [us] a bit younger and who were trying to find our stride. Matulka had a small school on 14 Street but maintained a rather secluded seriousness painting away on 89 St East as he still does. Stella often was around Romany Marie's but I did not think his work matched the monopoly discourse he preferred. Xceron was back and forth between Paris and New York and in Paris wrote art criticism for several American papers.

Our hangouts were Stewart's Cafeteria 7th Ave near 14 St close to Davis' studio and school and 5c coffee was much closer to our standards but on occasion we went to the Dutchman's, McSorley's and Romany Marie's. We followed Romany Marie from 8 St where Gorky once gave a chalk talk on Cubism, to several locations. Her place came closer to being a continental cafe with its varied types of professionals than any other place I knew. It was in Marie's where we once formed a group, Graham, Edgar Levy, Resnikoff, De Kooning, Gorky and myself with Davis being asked to join. This was short lived. We never exhibited and we lasted in union about 30 days. Our only action was to notify the Whitney Museum that we were a group and would only exhibit in the 1935 abstract show if all were asked. Some of us were, some exhibited, some didn't and that ended our group. But we were all what was then termed abstractionists.

_____

Dear Emanuel

About the Ironworks - I moved in early in '34. Two Irishmen Blackburn and Bushhorn owned the works, a ramshackle series of buildings on the Brooklyn waterfront at the foot of Atlantic Avenue.

Blackburn was a big, gentle ironmonger whose best expression was 'if you can't stick your foot in it, its flush'. Bushhorn was white collar, the job digger and check-writer, his was 'balls and six are eight'.

In '36 Blackburn sold to Bushhorn and took a job with Robbins drydock. In '39 Bushhorn sold and became a boiler inspector. Robert Henry the machinist a friend and fellow chess player went to a ship repair firm in Jersey City. Bushhorns father who had sold his Ivory Bone and Pearl works in lower Manhattan moved in with me as the

Terminal Bone and Pearl works and I was the Terminal Iron works. For several years we were ideal work mates each with seperate quarters. Bushhorn senior was a great craftsman - he had made revolver handles for as far back as Bill Cody. We worked hard drank our tea together, but the gaiety was gone

The Ironworks was inside the gates of the Atlantic Avenue Ferry terminal. George Kiernan who ran the 'men only' saloon at 13 Atlantic Avenue had inherited it, Indians in the window and all from his uncle Red Mike. We ate lunch got our mail and accepted it as a general community house. It was the social hall for blocks around. Any method or technique I needed, I could learn it from one of the habitues, and often got donated materials besides These were the depression days. My sculpture 'Blackburn' was made afterwards in homage. One called Bushhorn I will yet do.

Blackburn—Song of an Irish Blacksmith, steel/bronze, 1950

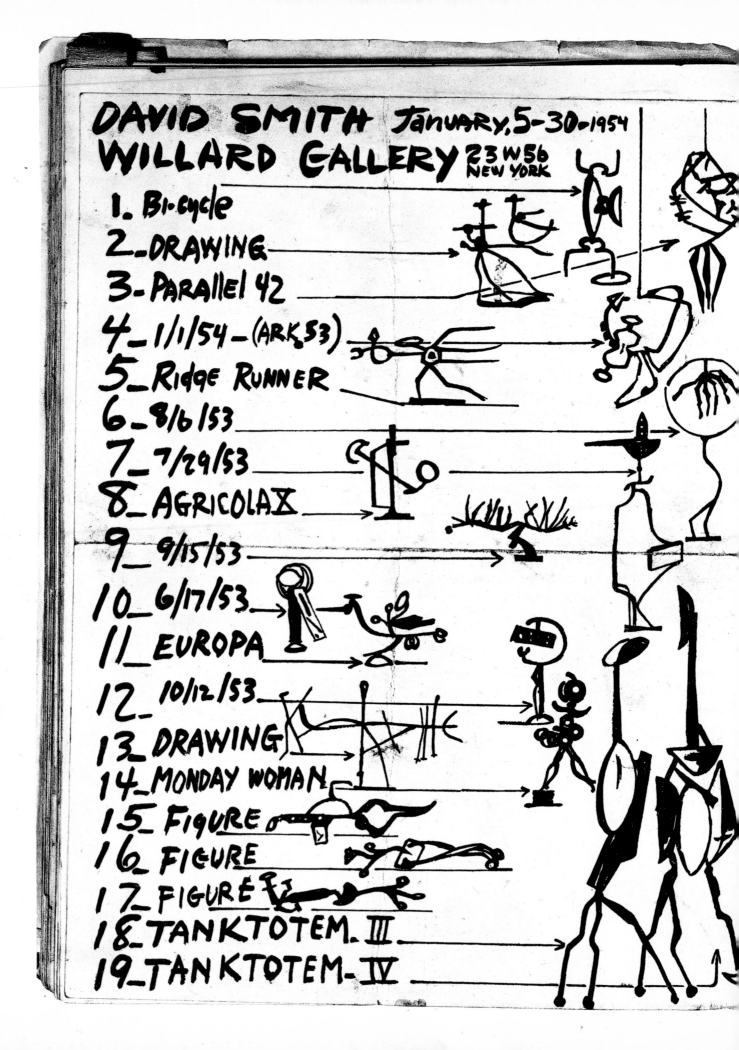

DAVID SMITH January, 5-30-1954
WILLARD GALLERY 23 W 56 NEW YORK

1. Bi-cycle
2. DRAWING
3. Parallel 42
4. 1/1/54 - (ARK 53)
5. Ridge Runner
6. 8/6/53
7. 7/29/53
8. AGRICOLA X
9. 9/15/53
10. 6/17/53
11. EUROPA
12. 10/12/53
13. DRAWING
14. MONDAY WOMAN
15. FIGURE
16. FIGURE
17. FIGURE
18. TANK TOTEM. III
19. TANK TOTEM. IV

My work day begins at 10 or 11 A. M. after a leisurely breakfast and an hour of reading. The shop is 800 ft. from the house. I carry my 2 P. M. lunch and return to the house at 7 for dinner. The work day ends from 1 to 2 A. M. with time out for coffee at 11:30. My shop here is called the Terminal Iron Works, since it closer defines my beginning and my method than to call it "studio."

At 11:30 when I have evening coffee and listen to WQXR on AM I never fail to think of the Terminal Iron Works at 1 Atlantic Ave., Brooklyn and the coffee pot nearby where I went same time, same station. The ironworks in Brooklyn was surrounded by all night activity—ships loading—barges refueling—ferries tied up at the dock. It was awake 24 hours a day, harbor activity in front, truck transports on Furman St. behind. In contrast the mountains are quiet except for occasional animal noises. Sometimes Streevers' hounds run foxes all night and I can hear them baying as I close up shop. Rarely does a car pass at night, there is no habitation between our road and the Schroon River 4 miles cross country. I enjoy the phenomenon of nature, the sounds, the Northern lights, stars, animal calls, as I did the harbour lights, tugboat whistles, buoy clanks, the yelling of men on barges around the T. I. W. in Brooklyn. I sit up here and dream of the city as I used to dream of the mountains when I sat on the dock in Brooklyn.

I like my solitude, black coffee and day dreams. I like the changes of nature, no two days or nights are the same. In Brooklyn what was nature was all man made and mechanical, but I like both, I like the companionship of music, I sometimes can get WNYC but always WQXR, Montreal, Vancouver or Toronto. I use the music as company in the manual labor part of sculpture of which there is much. The work flow of energy demanded by sculpture wherein mental exhaustion is accompanied by physical exhaustion, provides the only balance I've ever found, and as far as I know is the only way of life.

After 1 A. M., certain routine work has to be done, cleaning up, repairing machines, oiling, patining etc. I tune in WOR and listen to Nick's, Cafe Society, Eddie Condon's, whoever is on. After several months of good work, when I feel I deserve a reward, I go to N.Y., to concerts at YMHA, Gallery shows, museums, eat seafood, Chinese, go to Eddie's, Nick's, 6th Ave. Cafeteria, Artists Club, Cedar Tavern, run into late up artists, bum around chewing the fat, talk shop, finish up eating breakfast on 8th St. and ride it as hard and as long as I can for a few days, then back to the hills.

In the handwriting of Jean Smith:
*Rebecca's
first haircut
Feb. 1, 1957
David did it—
chintzy*

David Smith and Dorothy Dehner were divorced December 24, 1952
David Smith and Jean Freas were married April 6, 1953
Rebecca Smith was born April 4, 1954
Candida Smith was born August 12, 1955

Willard Gallery Exhibition, ink, 1954

CARNEGIE INSTITUTE
PITTSBURGH, PENNSYLVANIA, U.S.A.

At the Pittsburgh International Exhibition

of Contemporary Painting and Sculpture

held in the Art Galleries of the Carnegie Institute A. D. 19*61*.

Third Prize in Sculpture

was awarded to

David Smith

for

Zig IV

In attestation whereof the members of the Jury of Award have

hereto affixed their signatures.

President of Jury

Terminal Iron Works
Bolton Landing, New York
October 26, 1961
The Fine Arts Committee of
The Board of Trustees of
Carnegie Institute
c/o Mr. Gordon B. Washburn
4400 Forbes Avenue
Pittsburgh 13, Pennsylvania
Gentlemen:

I do not wish to accept the prize your guest jury has honored me with.

I wish the money involved returned to Institute direction, and I hope applied to use for purchase.

I believe the awards system in our day is archaic.

In my opinion all costs of jury, travel, miscellaneous expenses of the award machinery could be more honorably extended to the artist by purchase.

A few years ago I was chairman of a panel in Woodstock, New York, wherein the prize system was under discussion. The majority of artists spoke against the prize system. Dr. Taylor, then President of the Metropolitan Museum, was recognized as a speaker for the prize system. He spoke eloquently and defended this as of being the donor's prerogative and ended by summing up that the prize system is longstanding and honorable and goes back to the days of Ancient Rome when a prize was given for virginity. After the applause—a hand was raised for recognition by painter Arnold Blanch. His question— would the last speaker care to qualify the technical merits for second and third prize.

Thank you and greetings.

David Smith

Zig IV, steel painted, dated 7/7/61

I am writing a piece for Art in America as a sequel to Hyatt Mayor's article on good stamp design. It appears in an issue, separately mailed to you, on Page 32 under the title, "Stamps Designed by Fine Artists." To inform you about it further, we enclose a clipping from The New York Times.

Since the article created the most interesting results and even led the National Safety Council to ask Art in America whether artists might be requested to execute Commemorative Stamps for the United States Government, the idea spread to other fields, and I find myself as a result of this involved and interested in U. S. coins being similarly designed by outstanding American sculptors.

After some deliberation with representatives of Art in America, we are presenting the idea to the following sculptors and invite their design contribution for the various current and for some not yet existing coins: Calder for the penny; de Rivera for the nickel; Roszak, dime; Noguchi, a weightless aluminum 50 cent piece; Lipchitz, quarter; Smith, a stainless steel dollar; Lippold, a $25 gold piece.

It is planned to have plaster or wax models cast in the various metals (your model should probably be several times larger than the finished piece), and it may be possible to arrange a small display at the Guggenheim Museum showing these in the same manner in which stamp designs were presented at the Metropolitan Museum.

Mr. David Smith   -2-   July 16, 1962

It is our sincere hope that this may interest you and that you may wish to design the stainless steel dollar. I should add that, at this stage, it is the design idea rather than the ultimate execution that is on our minds, and that any lettering, etc., can be taken care of at the foundry. In order to complete this project on the existing schedule, plaster or wax designs would have to be in our hands by October 15, 1962, at the latest.

Let me add that I would be entirely at your disposal should you wish to call or write to me and that we would do everything possible to obtain your valuable participation.

Very sincerely yours,

Thomas M. Messer
Director

TMM:cy

Enclosure

I can share no enthusiasm for the administration who has no enthusiasm for art The administration than ~~~~ Mr Heckscher tours the country claiming affinity for the arts, but as I told Mr Hecksher at the recent Hofstra podium Art is painting and sculpture, not jazz bands and social musicals and the ~~Kennedy~~ administration has done no more for art than For you I'd like to ~~~~ — but for their cause it is a waste of time which I cannot afford. Which does not mean I voted for Nixon

David S

This draft of Smith's reply to Thomas Messer's letter was typed and mailed on July 31, 1962

41

As the result of a suggestion by Gian Carlo Menotti, Smith was invited during the summer of 1962 to work in Italy for the music festival at Spoletto. On this telegram, sent by the director of the factory where Smith was to make 26 sculptures in 28 days, Smith wrote the draft of his reply to the invitation

Beginning

The first Sunday alone in these factories, functional in an era long past, abandoned only a few months—were like Sundays in Brooklyn in 1934 at the Terminal Iron Works—except that here I could use anything I found—dragging parts between buildings to find their new identity. I thought of my Agricolas.[1] There was a similarity—but the language was different—and the size bolder. The first 2 Sundays, not even a skeleton crew around—the great quiet of stopped machines—the awe, the pull exceeded that of visits to museums in Genoa or even the ancient art in other cities. Part is personal heritage, part prejudice against connoisseurs' castles. Since we had identity, the desire to create excells over the desire to visit.

There is something quite middle class about ancient art in museums—choices by the order of scribes, fakes and gifts and rationalized purchases mix to one part with 99 parts destroyed or still uncovered.

My preference is ethnographic and archaeological.

Problem—Confront—

Day 1 to be introduced in white collar to my workmen, to whom I couldn't speak—awkward to us both—I've been them—In equal garb the next day—challenge—Request for swept floor not met. I swept floor. Request for moving of heavy objects not moved exact place. I move to positions. After welding, moving, sweeping, my collar was OK. We worked together from then on, great. An interpreter and unknown work added to the first problems but for only several days—we understood, and their desire to produce first class and to my need never failed.

Concentration

My own problems surmount the practical. To what degree of abstraction in concentration can one delve with noise and workmen who present other presences. My thoughts were often in creative vision during factory work. I've put in years at machines dreaming aesthetic ends—one never becomes oblivious to the surrounding order—in concentrated work alone under ideal conditions—outside vistas intrude like sex—hungers and assorted fears, fear in survival, lonesomeness for my children, many waves intrude during the most ideal set up—one works with one's nature—sets his own equilibrium, develops his resources, evens up his rage in whatever conditions present or the first hundred works would not have been set.

When elements like noise, others, dirt, grease enter the procedure they are but elements in nature more easily transposed than intruding mental pops. safety measures—machines—like any other conflict can be consumed and utilized towards complete concentration as any other conflict which one trips over.

Tongs on factory wall, Voltri, 1962

Group: *Voltri XI, Voltri VII, Voltri XXI*,
all steel, all dated 6/62

Voltri XV, steel, 1962

Workbenches

a factory stripped of its function, leaves on the floor from holes in the roof—quiet except for a bird cheep—from factory to factory I laid out workbenches—I finished two there, left more. I felt the awe and the scared air—like one returning survivor after holocaust—and as I had felt very young in Decatur when I went thru the window in my first abandoned factory. After the first shock of its immensity and the privilege, I felt at home, and then to work.

HOTEL COLUMBIA EXCELSIOR, GENOA, June 16 '62

My 8 workmen gave me 2 angel medallions (gold) with Rebecca and Candida's name engraved at the back—I'll get gold chains for them—they are not Catholic but Roman, such things touch me deeply —we had a close and fast relationship—to-day was 6 A. M. to 6 P. M. for all of us—they have been with me 7 days a week—we get along fine—they say they will miss me I say to them the same— the open and free feeling of sentiment is different than in the U.S. factory—afternoons each man brings a bottle of wine he made —pleasantries—kidding about the grade etc. are exchanged. One day we had snails—The man Cortezie [Cortesia] who brought them has a mother famous for her snails—they were the greatest I have ever had—of course wine bread salad all at 4 P. M.—another day Cova, a bird snatcher brot baby birds beautifully cooked—you eat bones and all—salad bread wine one day fresh anchovies—I'm soft in the heart for them & Italy.

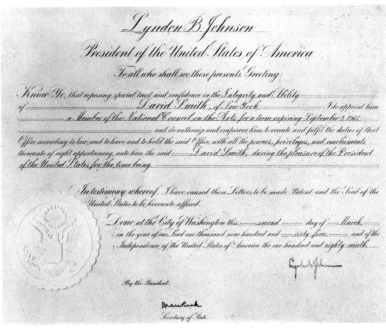

Certificate of appointment by President Lyndon Johnson to the National Council of the Arts. David Smith was the only artist on the Council

Pillar of Sunday, steel painted, 1945

Helmholtzian Landscape, steel painted, 1947

The Insect, steel burnished, 1948

The Royal Bird, steel/bronze/stainless steel, 1947—48

TECHNIQUE AND WORKING METHODS

My reverence for iron is in function before technique. It is
the cheapest metal. It conceptually is within the scale of my life.
And most important before I knew what art was I was an
ironmonger. The iron element I hold in high respect. I consider
it eidetic in property. The metal particularly possesses no art
craft. What it can do in arriving at form economically—no other
element can do.

The Shop, Bolton Landir

I worked in metal before I studied painting. When my painting developed into constructions leaving the canvas, I was then a sculptor, with no formal training in sculpture. When the constructions turned into metals, first lead, brass, and aluminum, combined with stone and coral in 1932, nothing technically was involved outside of factory knowledge. In the summer of 1933 I made the first group of iron sculptures (shown in this country?), two of which were exhibited in the winter of 1933 and spring of 1934. My first show in 1938 was comprised of work from 1935 on. This work was primarily gas welded. The first arc welded piece was made in 1939. My method of shaping material or arriving at form has been as functional as making a motor car or a locomotive. The equipment I use, my supply of material, come from what I learned in the factory, and duplicate as nearly as possible the production equipment used in making a locomotive. I have no aesthetic interest in tool marks, surface embroidery, or molten puddles. My aim in material function is the same as in locomotive building: to arrive at a given functional form in the most efficient manner. The locomotive method bows to no accepted theory of fabrication. It utilizes the respective merits of castings, forging, riveting, arc and gas welding, brazing, silver solder, bolts, screws, shrink fits, all because of their efficiency in arriving at an object or form in function. I make no claim for my work method over other media. It is not one of my private experience. It is one part of art that can definitely be taught or learned by the American aptitude for technics. A course in industrial high schools or an 8 week course in trade school suffices. The direct method, the part to the whole concept, quantity to quality, is not an exclusive approach, and does not exclude my use of other media.

A certain feeling for form will develop with technical skill, but imaginative form or aesthetic vision is not a guarantee for high technique. I have seen paper cut-outs that were finer art than piles of precious metals.

My own workshop is a small factory with the same make and quality tools used by production factories.

Steel . . . can be stainless, painted, lacquered, waxed, processed and electroplated with molybdenum. It can be cast. Steel has mural possibilities which have never been used. It has high tensile strength, pinnions can support masses, soft steel can bend cold, both with and across its grain, yet have a tensile strength of 30,000 lbs. to one square inch. It can be drawn, cupped, spun and forged. It can be cut and patterned by acetylene gas and oxygen and welded both electrically and by the acetylene oxygen process. It can be chiseled, ground, filed and polished. It can be welded the seams ground down leaving no evidence. The welds can possess greater strength than the parent metal. It can be formed with various metals by welding, brazing and soldering. Metals fall naturally to my use and [are] useful to my concept.

Between periods of trying to get an art education in three midwestern colleges I worked as a telephone linesman, stringing cable, laying cable, potting lead for joints etc. I used to dig holes in the ground of figures and form my own lead casts. I still like to, but in molds. After four months in department 346 at the Studebaker plant alternating on a lathe, spot welder and milling machine, I was transferred to 348 on Frame Assembly. This was worked on a group plan, payment made to 80 men in proportion to the completed frames which were riveted and assembled on an oval conveyor track. It was necessary for each man to be able to handle at least six operations. Riveting, drilling, stamping etc. all fell into my duties but my interest was the $45 to $50 per week which would enable me to study in New York. In a year I did, off and on for five years. Painted 5 years. Years ago while working on constructions of various materials in aluminum, stone, brass etc. I realized the inadequacy of their strength was apparent when trying to make them conform; as a result I turned to steel.

The medium has been used by Gonzalez and Gargallo and others. Both men have used it in an abstracted manner from a personalized viewpoint. The mental process and the metal both take shape in [an] abstract point of view. The objects I had worked with in the factory were abstract. They were always functional pieces, having relationships but were not objects of realism, gears, cross members, brackets, the triangle in a circle, spare tire carrier etc. were all abstract parts.

This work with abstract mechanical parts did not consciously exert their influence on an abstract concept developed from realism. It resulted in a concept recalling the use of the material.

I work in most media, but my especial material is steel, that which has been longest in my experience, and which seems to me unique in sculptural media. The metal possesses little art history. Its associations are primarily of this century. It is structure, movement, progress, suspension, cantilever and at times destruction and brutality. Its method of unity need not be evident. Yet its forms of geometry, planes, hard lines are all constant with the that of my time. Altho material is always subservient to concept, certain properties of this material are unique and have not existed before this century.

In my own procedure, along with the material, a new concept process has developed. That is where the distant whole or finished work consists of the sum of its parts. This is much like the industrial method of building a machine but without a blueprint, and where the function is only visual. Where the end is never seen until the final part, and the finality being realized when each part in unity works up to the whole. Conceptually this procedure is much like painting. The sculptural entity never takes place until summed up by its parts.

Romantically speaking, the indication of form by bulk mass does not possess its old validity. Mass is energy. Space is energy. Nothing is without energy. Nothing is without mass. The indication of area or pattern is a statement of energy and as sculptural as sculpture can be. Certain changes in scientific speculation act in poetic considerations that become working constants in artistic consideration.

To me it is impossible to conceive 2 dimensions. I have seen a Chinese granite carving in the Boston Museum and found its depth to be less than the thickness of paint in paintings by both Van Gogh and Cézanne. Validities and designations become inactive. The limitations are mental. When poetic considerations change, the audience must be willing to soar with the artist or stay behind.

The conceptual premises limiting sculpture to dead white marble and fragmentary concept, or to the monolithic no longer applies, the sculptor's world is one of vision with no conception barred. You cannot expect sculpture to have any limits.

I follow no set procedure in starting a sculpture. Some works start out as chalk drawings on the cement floor with cut steel forms working into the drawings. When it reaches the stage that the structure can become united, it is welded into position upright. Then the added dimension requires different considerations over the more or less profile form of the floor drawing assembly.

Sometimes I make a lot of drawings using possibly one relationship in each drawing which will add up in the final work. Sometimes sculptures just start with no drawing at all. This was the case of "The Fish" which is some 6' high and about five feet long.

I have two studios. One clean, one dirty, one warm, one cold. The house studio contains drawing tables, etching press, cabinets for work record, photos and drawing paper stock. The shop is a cinder block structure transite roof and full row of North windows skylights set at a 30 degree angle. With heat in each end it is usable to zero weather.

I do not resent the cost of the best material or the finest tools and equipment. Every labor saving machine, every safety device I can afford I consider necessary. Stocks of bolts, nuts, taps, dies, paints, solvents, acids, protective coatings, oils, grinding wheels, polishing discs, dry pigments, waxes, chemicals, spare machine parts, are kept stocked on steel shelving, more or less patterned after a factory stockroom.

Sheets of stainless steel, bronze, copper, aluminum are stocked in 1/8" × 4' × 8' are stocked for fabricating cold and hot rolled 4' × 8' sheets are stacked outside the shop in thickness from 1/8" to 7/8". Lengths of strips, shapes and bar stock are racked in the basement of the house or interlaced in the joists of the roof. Maybe I brag a bit about my stock, but it is larger since I've been on a Guggenheim Fellowship that it ever has been before. I mention this not because it has anything to do with art, but it indicates how important it is to have material on hand, that the aesthetic vision is not limited by material need.

The cost problem I have to forget on everything, because it is always more than I can afford,—more than I get back from sales, most years more than I earn. My shop is somewhat like the Federal Government always running with greater expenditures than income and winding up with loans.

The Cathedral (4 stages of construction), steel welded, 1950

When I begin a sculpture I am not always sure how it is going to end. In a way it has a relationship to the work before, it is in continuity to the previous work—it often holds a promise or a gesture towards the one to follow.

I do not often follow its path from a previously conceived drawing. If I have a strong feeling about its start, I do not need to know its end, the battle for solution is the most important. If the end of the work seems too complete, and final, posing no question, I am apt to work back from the end, that in its finality it poses a question and not a solution. Sometimes when I start a sculpture, I begin with only a realized part, the rest is travel to be unfolded much in the order of a dream. The conflict for realization is what makes art not its certainty, nor its technique or material. I do not look for total success. If a part is successful the rest clumsy or incomplete, I can still call it finished, if I've said anything new by finding any relationship which I might call an origin. I will not change an error if it feels right, for the error is more human than perfection.

When it [the sculpture] is finished there is always that time when I am not sure—it is not that I am not sure of my work, but I have to keep it around for months to become acquainted with it and sometimes it is as if I've never seen it before and as I work on other pieces and look at it all the kinship returns, the battle of arriving, its relationship to the preceding work and its relationship to the new piece I am working on. Now comes the time when I feel very sure of it, that it is as it must be and I am ready to show it to others and be proud I made it.

Editions duplication

Since the artist's job is the extension of his concept by successive new works, duplication does not help—because its time robs new work concepts. If he is involved, each duplication occupies a niche in his consciousness—and identifies him with commercialism when he should be battling with his own aesthetic truth.

If this is a debatable point, my answer is that one should then be in the production business, preferably on an item that can have greater distribution.

An artist should be selfish to concept, morally—ethically and practically. I do not believe in reproductions or editions of sculpture for us. Let us not cite history. Our logic and time is now. Our own truth as the artist is our dominant identity. I see no collective ideals, nothing outside personal truth to identify with.

We have no clients, no clients' preferences. We also have no excuses—and mostly we earn our own way at work other than sculpture.

The accent must always be on concept over casting and I refuse any discourse on technics alone. This belongs to the foundry journal.

What do you want from bronze—to perpetuate the ruling class connotation idols—that if it's bronze it's art.

I wouldn't like to see sculpture become a craft—and like etching a reproductive process—sculpture is a conceptual process—and needs not bronze—but sticks and stones rags and bones—depending upon the artist's conviction

If I make a cast sculpture, I make one; and all the marks are mine. I don't approve of copies and I don't make and produce copies for the sake of making more money.

There are minor things that relate to our time now that are changing. I am personally interested in a man made object. Now because this is a productive age and it is more unique there is freshness of origin. If I am making a sculpture I wish to have just as much integrity as a painter. I want to make one image, I want to have controlled every make in it. I am not the least bit interested in having one image and having it cast in reproductions . . . The idea seemed to be that you make art and spread it out to a lot of different people. I think that people should spread themselves and go to the museum where the art is.

There are certain economic conditions which make it necessary when possible for the sculptor to control the total processing of his work of art. Outside of aesthetics, the labor and production costs are equal or higher than the sculptor's own wage.

I have never conceived a work of art in other than the material demanded by that intention. An intermediate stage of pattern, with unrealized casting has always gnawed at my soul. I have hundreds of sculptures on paper which time and conceptual change have passed by. If I were ten people and had the production cost they might be realized. Even as it is the production costs force limits in scale, material and output. But if I were working in plaster or wax for art foundry casting the output would be but half of my present.

define technique

technique is what belongs to others

technique is what others call it when
you have become successful at it

technique as far as you are concerned
is the way others have done it

technique is nothing you can speak about
when you are doing it

it is the expectancy of impostors

                they do not show a
                respect for themselves
                or for what they are doing

It takes belligerent conviction to make art. The artist usually must earn his living and the cost of his materials by means other than the sale of his work. He must express alone and rationalize his whole life to that end. Contemporary sculpture is expensive to make, difficult to exhibit and not easy to sell. The sculptor wishes more people liked his work well enough to buy it—not because he wants wealth but because he needs money to make more sculpture. But the fact that it doesn't come out this way doesn't make him change his profession or doubt his concept. It just means that less sculpture gets made while he earns his survival outside his studio.

Points of finance and public rejection add nothing to the process but a little to the concept—explaining the seeming belligerence of the artist to society and the demi-devotees. For most art is produced despite society and not by its aid.

True understanding or projection of the receptor's vision in an attempt to follow the creative process which made the work of art is very rare. The effort is too great for the minds degraded by current propaganda, pre-digested reading—the world of banal moving images.

From the artist's point of view he deals with truths, statements of reality—involved in the state of pure freedom individual freedom images outside of the creative field—this is not current practice in our culture.

Only artists understand art—possibly because one artist can go along with another artist the path he followed in creating it.

By choice I identify myself with workingmen and still belong to Local 2054 United Steelworkers of America. I belong by craft—yet my subject of aesthetics introduces a breach. I suppose that it is because I believe in a workingman's society in the future and in that society I hope to find a place. In this society I find little place to identify myself economically.

I have strong social feelings. I do now. And about the only time I was ever able to express them in my work was when I made a series of medallions which were against the perils or evils of war, against inhuman things. They were called "Medals for Dishonor.". . . It was about the only thing I have ever done which contributed with my work to a social protest. I don't feel I have to protest with my work. Whatever society I belong to must take me for my ability; my effort is to drive to the fullest extent those few talents that were given me, and propaganda is not necessarily my forte.

There is nothing here but art
the product of the artist
It is not the artisan adaptation
so long demanded by society
So much required by the most degenerate czars
the treasures of Vienna, the popes the kings
the tycoons, the advertising accounts
the revolt started before
but it is still revolt when carried through in context
_____
defiance of all power that demands artisan
performance by the artist
revolt against material function
demanding full right for the function of pure aesthetics

Royal Incubator, steel/bronze, 1949

Portrait of the Eagle's Keeper, bronze, 1949

Egyptian Landscape, steel/bronze painted, 1951

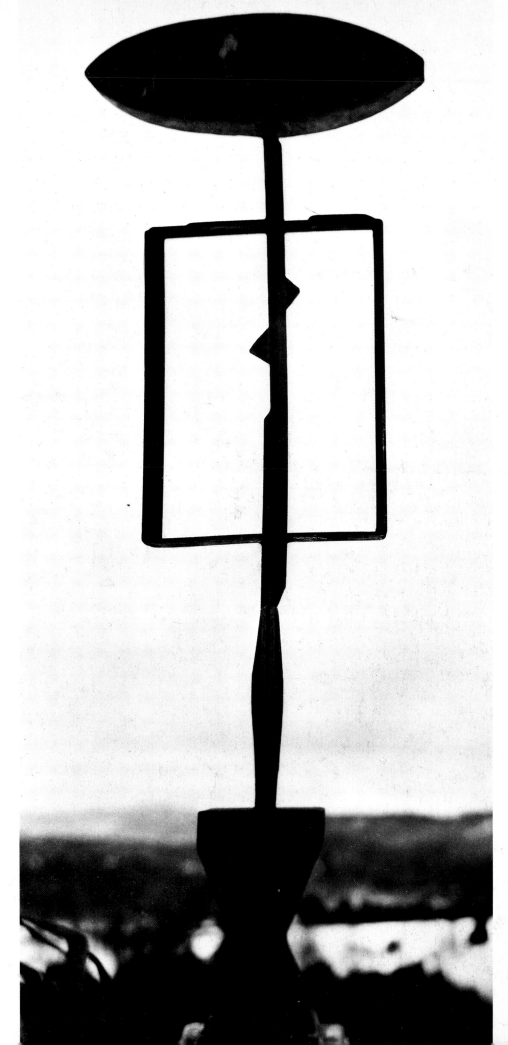

The Hero, steel, 1952

THE CONCEPT OF VISION

Everything imagined is reality
The mind cannot conceive unreal things

Australia, steel, 1951

After my student period in painting finishing with the abstract painter Jan Matulka, my painting had turned to constructions which had risen from the canvas so high that a base was required where the canvas should be, I now was a sculptor.

I had seen the Picasso-Gonzalez iron constructions of 1931 in the magazine Cahier d'Art. This was the liberating factor which permitted me to start with steel which before had been my trade, and had until now only meant labor and earning power for the study of painting.

My first steel sculptures were made in 1933. They were partly made from found objects, agricultural machine parts of past function. To a relative degree they relate to my Agricola series, thirteen pieces of this group having been completed within the past two years.

My work of 34, 35, 36 was often referred to as line sculpture. My first show in 1938 included this work with the balance being painted planal constructions.

I have always considered line contour as being a comment on mass space and more acute than bulk, and that the association of steel retained steel function of shapes moving, circumscribing upon axis, moving and gearing against each other at different speeds, as the association of this material suggests.

The overlay of line shapes, being a cubist invention, permits each form its own identity and when seen thru each other highly multiplies the complex of associations into new unities.

I do not accept the monolithic limit in the tradition of sculpture. Sculpture is as free as the mind, as complex as life . . .

Some critics refer to certain pieces of my sculpture as "two-dimensional." Others call it "line drawing." I do not admit to this, either conceptually or physically. It may be true in part, but only as one attribute of many, and that by intention and purpose. There are no rules in sculpture. This particular criticism is not sufficient or valid grounds for dismissal.

I make no apologies for my end-views. They are as important as they are intended to be. If a sculpture could be a line drawing, then speculate that a line drawing removed from its paper bond and viewed from the side would be a beautiful thing, one which I would delight in seeing in the work of other artists. The end-view or profile of an interesting person or object arouses the mind to completion of the imagined personality and physiognomy, since a work of art or an object of interest is always completed by the viewer and is never seen the same by any two persons.

Stainless Window, stainless steel, 1951

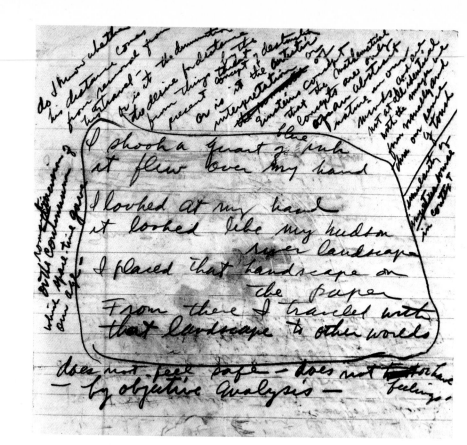

I shook a quart of ink
it flew over my hand

I looked at my hand
it looked like my hudson
                    river landscape
I placed that landscape on
                    the paper
From there I traveled with
that landscape to other worlds

Hudson River Landscape, steel, 1951

In my own work I maintain that I deal with realities. These realities are my own choice and are never one, or exist alone. Although the point of departure may be identifiable, the trip it takes in the mind, its attributes, its associations are still within the orbit I choose to call reality. For instance, a recent work called "Hudson River Landscape," started from drawings made on a train between Albany and Pough-keepsie, a synthesis of drawings from 10 trips going and coming over this 75 mile stretch. On this basis I started a drawing for a sculpture. As I began, I shook a quart bottle of India ink, it flew over my hand, it looked like my landscape. I placed my hand on paper and from the image this left I travelled with the landscape to other landscapes and their objects, with additions, deductions, directives which flashed past too fast to tabulate, but whose elements are in the finished sculpture. No part is diminished reality, the total is a unity of symbolized reality, which to my mind is greater reality than the river scene. Is my work, "Hudson River Landscape," the Hudson River, or is it the travel, the vision, the ink spot, or does it matter? The sculpture exists on its own, it is the entity. The name is an affectionate designation of the point prior to travel. My objective was not these words, or the Hudson River, but to create the existence of a sculpture. Your response may not travel down the Hudson River but it may travel on any river or on a higher level . . .

Sculpture is a poetic statement of form. The forward sculptor deals with nature, but his nature has changed from the bowl of fruit, the nude and the cloaked figure of virtue to new discoveries in nature. Today the landscape may be viewed on a cross country journey from a plane three miles up. Looking down there is no space. The solid earth, its rocks and hills become an endless flat plane. Houses, factories, hard objects, solids become only pattern. Rivers, highways, man-made boundaries are flowing graceful sweeping lines opposed by spots of lakes and squares of fields. The view from space makes solid form appear pattern.

The impressionist painter Pissarro might have liked this 3-mile view in space, for from his ground position he once said: "Do not fix your eye on any one point, but take in everything, observing how colors reflect their surroundings . . . work at the same time sky, water, branches and ground, keeping everything going on an equal basis." What was a poetic working principle for Pissarro has become an actual view in space for us today, to be accented differently. Sculpture isn't made from 3 miles up, but pattern and line to represent form are working on equal basis in contemporary expression.

In contemporary work, force, power, ecstasy, structure, intuitive accident, statements of action dominate the object. Or they power the object with belligerent vitality. Probably the fact that man the artist can make works of art direct without the object meets opposition by its newness. Possibly this direct approach is a gesture of revolt representing the new freedom, unique in our time. Possibly there is a current ecstasy in the artist's new position much like that of 1910–12 Cubism.

From the artist there is no conscious effort to find universal truth or beauty, no effort to analyze other men's minds in order to speak for them. His act in art is an act of personal conviction and identity. If there is truth in art, it is his own truth. If beauty is involved, it is only the metaphor of imagination.

The metaphor of a symbol—the symbol of a symbol of a symbol—and in a chess game—how many plays ahead can you realize?

The "Fish" in the Whitney Show is part of both the scales of vertebra, the schools of, the force of one equally using the other, the first fish who walked, the first fish who flew, the first fish who was man. I made it, I view in perspective both the fish and man and attributes.

The Fish, steel painted, 1950

"h's"—"y's"—"Birdheads"—"The Letter"
before the alphabet letters made words, they
should have been symbols which made the object real by abstracting.
Depiction of objects were identity memories
requiring the ability of the artist—before words
were joined to be degenerated by the moralists
pragmatists and sect-educators.
I have brought identity by symbols in
varying relationships to be approached visually—
back to the symbol origin
demanding your recall

The motives of celebration of beauties like "Star Cage," "The
Forest," and "Songs of the Landscape"—such celebrations
are evolved in "Sacrifice," "The Cathedral," "The Letter" are
compassion, hates, fears and are melancholy songs
about traps [in] which evolutionary involvement
and chance envelop us, ensnare many of us, cause us to
ensnare ourselves

The Letter, steel welded, 1950

Sacrifice, steel welded, 1950

Agricola VIII, steel/cast iron, 8/1952

Forms in function are often not appreciated in their context except for their mechanical performance. With time and the passing of these functions and a separation of their parts, a metamorphic change can take place permitting a new unity, one that is strictly visual.

The Agricola series are new unities whose parts are related to past tools of agriculture.

For how long does it take crudities to become beauties?

Agricola IX, steel, 8/1952

Thoughts travel and come unexpectedly rarely down the same path—
I was drinking beer with Kannemitsui one evening—he mentioned studying
with Zadkine—my thoughts saw concave convex—and the sculpture I had
recently finished called Bouquet of Concaves, and immediately my vision
grew to concaves larger than my own being, and on a piece of cardboard,
I made a unity of concaves in orders I had not found in my previous
concaves—they shined—and the material demanded stainless steel—which
I have now started to put into work. This was a flash of recognition related
to my previous work yet a reference atmosphere existed in the filial history
of Zadkine. And after that appreciatively recalled Léger in 1913 like the
pictures of so called Tubism in the Arensberg collection in Philadelphia.

Bouquet of Concaves, steel painted, 1959

When ~~you~~ I see a good sculpture
there are ~~images~~ actions before ~~its presence~~
there are images after —

This is but part of the imaginative
reference aroused a good work &
if your sensibilities are tuned

Art isn't made for the wealthy
it comes from the life of the
artist — out of his own life
his own ~~environment~~ environment

My sculpture and especially my drawings relate to my past works, the 3 or 4 works in progress and to the visionary projection of what the next sculptures are to be. One of these projections is to push beauty to the very edge of rawness. To push beauty and imagination farther towards the limits of accepted state, to keep it moving and to keep the edge moving, to shove it as far as possible towards that precipitous edge where beauty balances but does not topple over the edge of the vulgar.

The term "vulgar" is a quality, the extreme to which I want to project form, and it may be society's vulgarity, but it is my beauty. The celebrations, the poetic statement in the form of cloud-longing is always menaced by brutality. The cloud-fearing of spectres has always the note of hope, and within the vulgarity of the form an upturn of beauty. Despite the subject of brutality, the appreciation must show love. The rape of man by war machine will show the poetic use of form in its making. The beauties of nature do not conceal destruction and degeneration. Form will flower with spikes of steel, the savage idols of basic patterns. The point of departure will start at departure. The metaphor will be the metaphor, of a metaphor, and then totally oppose it.

If the vitality is there the shape will grow form

The quality of vitality I feel comes first— other orders follow.

Perfection
It always surprises me but where art comes from is spiritually much closer to the dump and discard of the culture.

Provincialism or coarseness or unculture is greater for creating art than finesse or polish. Creative art has a better chance of developing from coarseness and courage than from culture. One of the good things about American art is that it doesn't have the spit and polish that some foreign art has. It is coarse. One of its virtues is coarseness. A virtue can be anything, as long as that conviction projects an origin—and free as courage. As long as it has the fire, I don't think it matters, because there are all kinds of qualities in art, and I'm not very involved in the differentiation or the qualitative value of who has what in art. I would much rather have a man who has no ideals in art, but who has tremendous drive about it with the fire to make it.

Very often I seem to be much more concerned with the monsters than with what are called beauties . . . I don't feel at all like the age of graces. I like girls, but I don't feel at all like using that feminine grace in concepts . . . I don't think this is an age of grace.

Beauty is to expose the cruelty in men

77

They can begin with any idea. They can begin with a found object, they can begin with no object, they can begin sometimes even when I'm sweeping the floor and I stumble and kick a few parts that happen to throw into an alignment that sets me off in thinking and sets off a vision of how it would finish if it all had that kind of accidental beauty to it. I want to be like a poet, in a sense.

Photographs taken by Smith and found in his miscellaneous file.

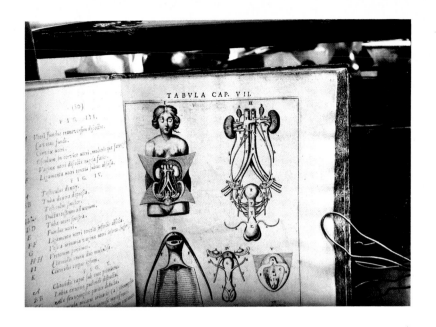

Group: *3 Forgings,* steel, 1955; *Yellow Vertical,* steel painted, 1955;
The Woman Bandit, steel/cast iron/bronze, 1955; *Forging,* steel painted, 1955

Group: *Tank Totem IV,* steel, 1953; *Untitled,* steel painted, 1953;
Tank Totem III, steel, 1953

Tank Totem V, steel, 1953–56

The Five Spring, steel/nickel/stainless steel, 1956

NOTEBOOKS, DRAWINGS, PAINTINGS

Drawing is the most direct, closest to the true self,
the most natural celebration of man—and if I may guess, back
to the action of very early man, it may have been the first
celebration of man with his secret self—even before song.

Living room floor, Bolton Landing, 1959

Even the drawing made before the performance is often greater, more truthful, more sincere than the formal production later made from it. Such a statement will find more agreement with artists than from connoisseurs. Drawings are usually not pompous enough to be called works of art. They are often too truthful. Their appreciation neglected, drawings remain the life force of the artist.

Especially is this true for the sculptor who, of necessity, works in media slow to take realization, and where the original creative impetus must be maintained during labor, drawing is the fast moving search which keeps physical labor in balance.

Nude, ink/pencil, 1933–45

I don't make boy sculptures. They become kind of personages, and sometimes they cry out to me that I should have been better or bigger, and mostly they tell me that I should have done that twelve years before—or twenty years before.

Four Nudes, ink/color, 1946

Iron Woman, steel painted, 1957

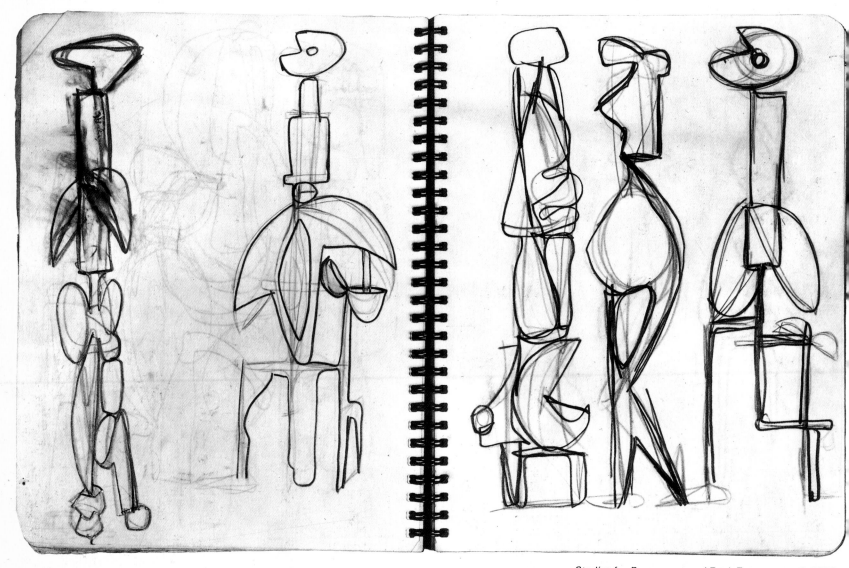

Studies for Personages and Tank Totems, pencil, 1952

The drawing that comes from the serious hand can be unwieldy, uneducated, unstyled and still be great simply by the superextension of whatever conviction the artist's hand projects, and being so strong that it eclipses the standard qualities critically expected. The need, the drive to express can be so strong that the drawing makes its own reason for being.

Group: *History of Le Roy Burton*, steel, 1956; *Portrait of a Painter*, bronze, 1956; *The Sitting Printer*, bronze, 1955

Group: *Personage of August*, steel, 1957; *Sentinel I*, stainless steel, 1958;
Running Daughter (unfinished), steel painted, 1956–60;
Tank Totem VI, steel painted, 1958; *Sentinel II*, stainless steel, 1957;
Pilgrim, iron/steel painted, 1957

Three Personages, pencil, 1952–54

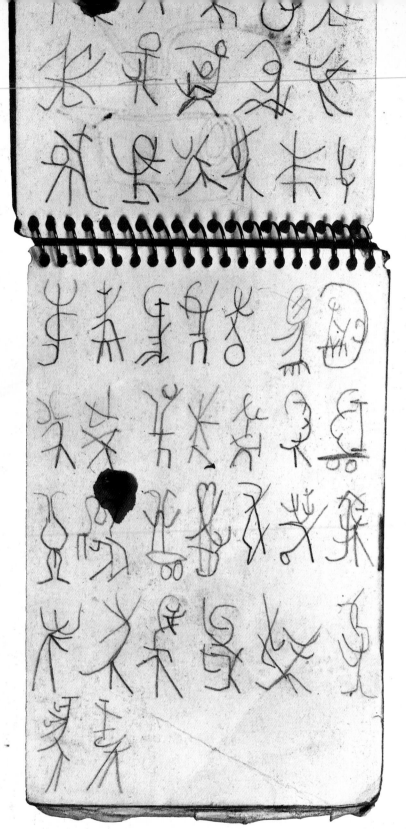

Imaginary Glyphs, ink, 1952–54

Study in Arcs, steel, previously dated 1949 but more likely mid-1950's

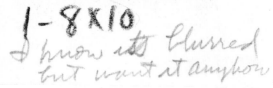

J-8X10
I know its blurred
but want it anyhow

Running Daughter, steel painted, 1956–60

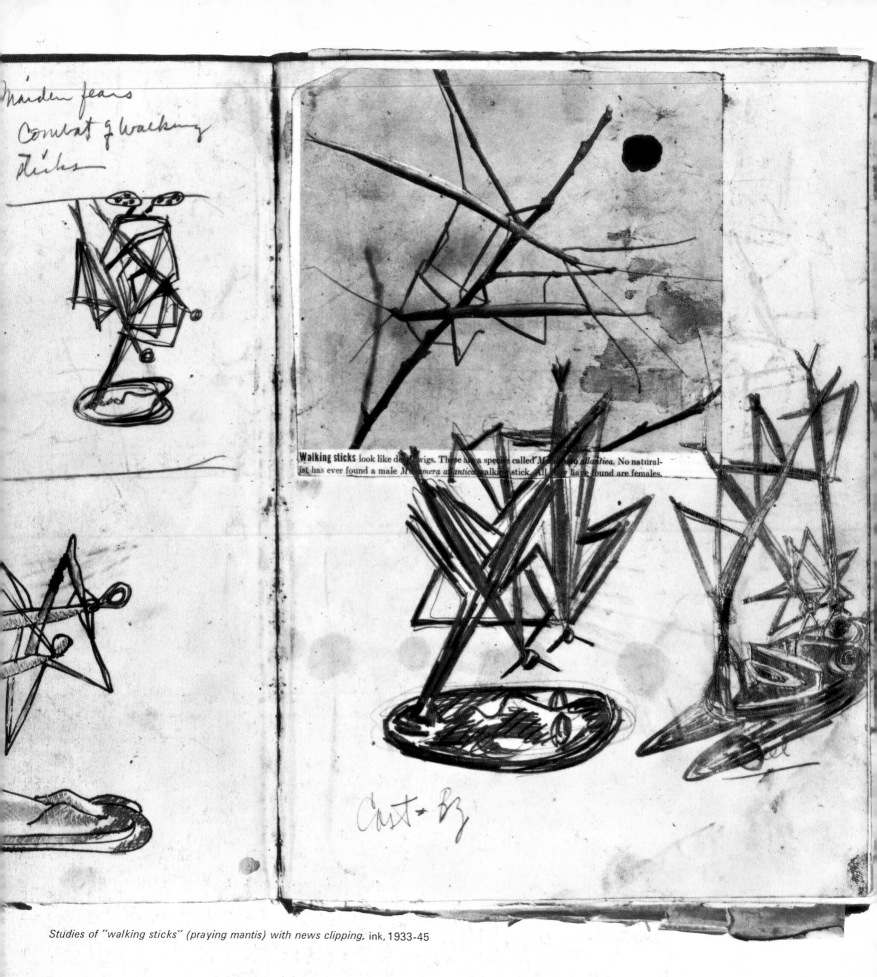

Maiden fears
Combat of walking
sticks

Walking sticks look like dead twigs. These are a species called *Manomera atlantica*. No naturalist has ever found a male *Manomera atlantica* walking stick. All they have found are females.

Cast = Bz

Studies of "walking sticks" (praying mantis) with news clipping, ink, 1933-45

The Maiden's Dream, bronze, 1949

The Jurassic Bird, steel, 1945

Bird Skeletons, ink, 1944–54

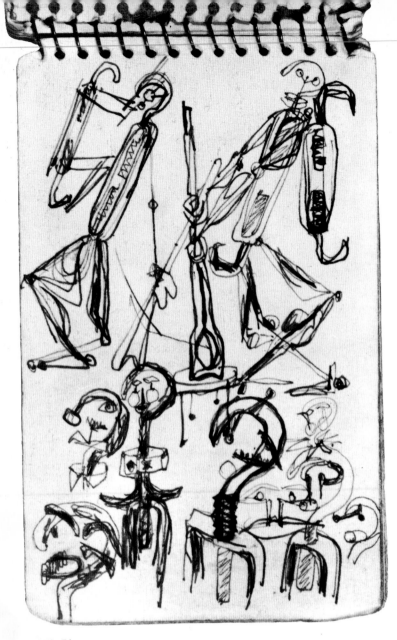

Studies for Four Soldiers, ink, 1951

Four Soldiers, steel/stainless steel, 1950–51

100

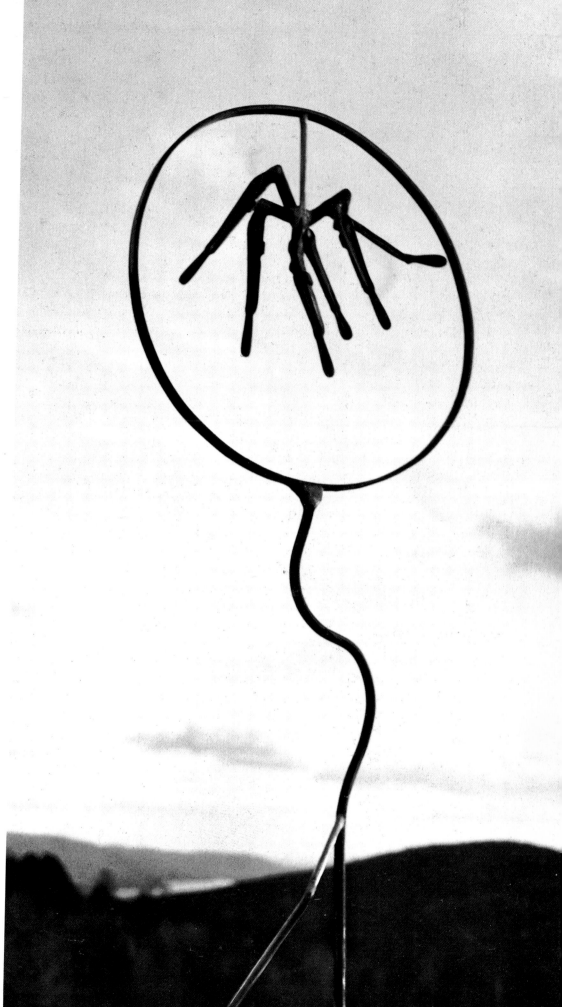

8/6/53, steel/stainless steel, 1953

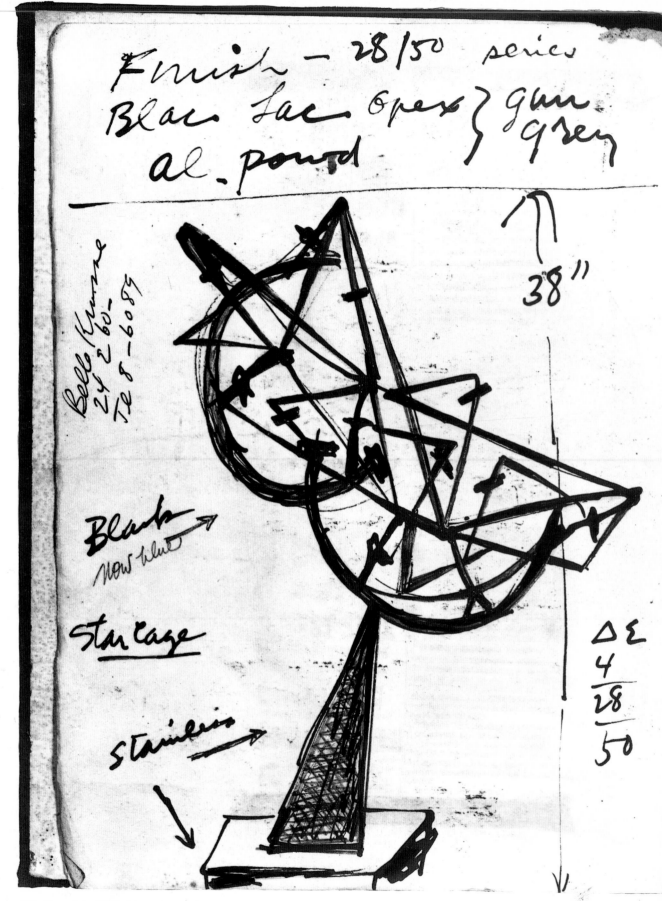

Finish - 28/50 series
Blac Lac Opex } gun
al _ pond } grey

Bell Krume
24 2.60-
Te 8-6089

38"

Black →
now blue

Star Cage

Stainless →

$\Delta \varepsilon$
4
28
50

Star Cage, ink, 1950–54

Star Cage, stainless steel painted, 1950

I make 300 to 400 large drawings a year, usually with egg yolk and Chinese ink and brushes. These drawings are studies for sculpture, sometimes what sculpture is, sometimes what sculpture can never be. Sometimes they are atmospheres from which sculptural form is unconsciously selected during the labor process of producing form. Then again they may be amorphous floating direct statements in which I am the subject, and the drawing is the act. They are all statements of my identity and come from the constant work stream. I title these drawings with the numerical noting of month day and year. I never intend a day to pass without asserting my identity; my work records my existence.

Drawing, ink, *c.* 1959

Tower I, stainless steel, 1962–63   105

I belong with painters, in a sense; and all my early friends were painters because we all studied together. And I never conceived of myself as anything other than a painter because my work came right through the raised surface and color and objects applied to the surface. Some of the greatest contributions to sculpture of the 20th century are by painters. Had it not been for painters, sculpture would be in a very sorry position . . . Some of the greatest departures in the concept of sculpture have been made by Picasso and Matisse. There was a series of heads that Matisse made called . . . Jeanette; in there are some of the very brilliant departures in the concept of sculpture. Painting and sculpture aren't very far apart.

I painted for some years. I've never given it up; I always, even if I'm having trouble with a sculpture, I always paint my troubles out.

Group of paintings, *c.* 1959

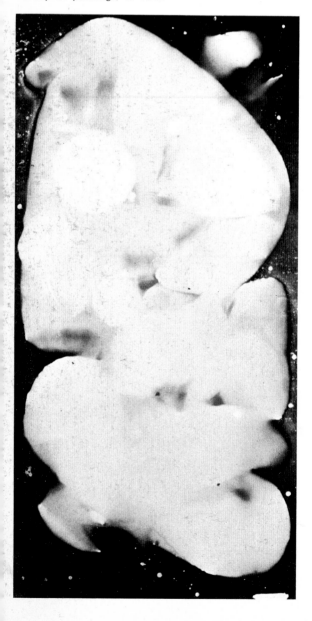  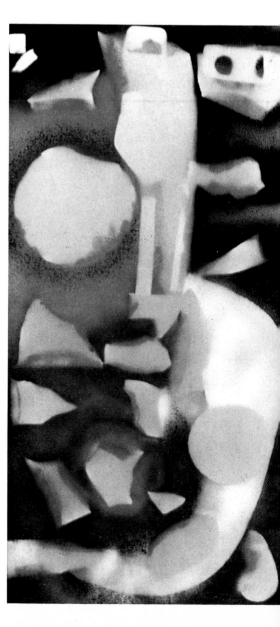

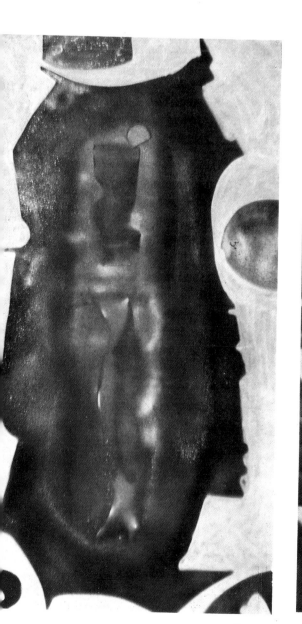

Lunar Arcs on 1 Leg, steel painted, 1956–60

Timeless Clock, silver, 1957

Four Units Unequal, stainless steel, 1960

Lectern Sentinel, stainless steel, 1961

COLOR

The april beauty of true color
before it's struck with green

Zig II, steel painted, 1961

It would be easier to state color in a gentle monochrome manner, except it doesn't speak to me as strongly. I could work whites and blacks, but I think I'd have to work 20 years before I can paint circles in bright colors that succeed, and the minute I'd succeed, I would be done; that would be ended.

Circle II, steel painted, 1962

When you ask the question to black—is it white, is it day or night, good or evil, positive or negative, is it life or death, is it the superficial scientific explanation about the absence of light; is it a solid wall or is it space, is it paint, a man, a father, or does it come out blank having been censored out by some unknown or unrecognizable association? There is no one answer. Black is no one thing. The answer depends upon impression. The importance of what black means depends upon your conviction and your artistic projection of black; depends upon your poetic vision, your mythopoetic view, your myth of black. And to the creative mind the dream and myth of black is more the truth of black than the scientific theory or the dictionary explanation or the philosopher's account of black. Black—as a word, as an image recall flashes past too fast for any rational word record—but its imagery is all involved or used by selection by the artist when he uses black on a brush.

Wagon I, steel painted, 1964

Tank Totem IX, steel painted, 8/30/60

I color them. They are steel, so they have to be protected, so if you have to protect them with a paint coat, make it color. Sometimes you deny the structure of steel. And sometimes you make it appear with all its force in whatever shape it is. No rules . . .

I've been painting sculpture all my life. As a matter of fact, the reason I became a sculptor is that I was first a painter.

The paint here is not artist's paint. It is auto enamel, and I mix it and it is much better than artist's paint for outdoors. First the iron is ground down so that it is raw, and it is painted with about 15 coats of epoxy primer and then a few coats of zinc—and then a few coats of white—and then the color is put on. So it runs about 25 or 30 coats and that's about 3 times the paint coat on a Mercedes or about 30 times the paint coat on a Ford or Chevrolet. And if it doesn't get scratched or hammered I think the paint coat will last longer than I do. There is nothing better for outside painting than auto enamel as far as I know.

Sometimes I need total disrespect for the material and paint it as if it were a building.

119

The red of rust has a higher value to me than antiquity relationship. It is the metal of terra rasa, ochre, Indian red, the Mars group etc. It is the order of time—natural destruction, oxidation. It is intrinsic growth—four parts rust are 2 parts iron 2 parts oxygen. Its susceptibility to this eventual theoretic destruction is the means by which it is refined—and most easily controlled to shape (oxy-acetylene cutting). It is the red of the east's mythical west. It is the blood of man, it was preculture symbol of life.

Voltri-Bolton IV, steel, 12/3/62

I like outdoor sculpture and the most practical thing for outdoor sculpture is stainless steel, and I make them and I polish them in such a way that on a dull day, they take on the dull blue, or the color of the sky in the late afternoon sun, the glow, golden like the rays, the colors of nature. And in a particular sense, I have used atmosphere in a reflective way on the surfaces. They are colored by the sky and the surroundings, the green or blue of water. Some are down by the water and some are by the mountains. They reflect the colors. They are designed for outdoors.

Group: *Cubi XVIII*, 2/19/64; *Cubi XVII*, 12/4/63; *Cubi XIX*, 2/20/64, all stainless steel

123

Color adds another challenge. And I don't like pretty colors. I like kind of raw colors . . . I've just now got some real nice, rough, raw colors—once in a while that is—but not so good as I will get . . . My idea of color, for me, is real gutty.

Tank Totem X. steel painted, 1960

This is the only time, in these stainless steel pieces, that I have been able to utilize light and I depend upon the reflective power of light . . . it does have a semi-mirror reflection and I like it in that sense because no other material in sculpture can do that.

11 Books 3 Apples, stainless steel, 1958

Group: *Primo Piano III*, steel painted, 1962;
Primo Piano II, steel painted, 1962

Group: *Tank Totem VII*, steel painted, 1960; *Noland's Blues, Rebecca Circle, Ninety Father, Ninety Son;* all steel painted, 1961

Circle I, steel painted, 1962

Circle III, steel painted, 1962

HISTORY AND TRADITION

Culture and the ideal of perfection is the refinement which
belongs to gentle men—art is the raw stuff which
comes from the vitality, labor of aggressiveness by men who
got that way fighting for survival.

Shop Exterior, Bolton Landing, *c.* 1960

I believe that my time is the most important in the world. That the art of my time is the most important art. That the art before my time has no immediate contribution to my aesthetics since that art is history explaining past behaviour, but not necessarily offering solutions to my problems. Art is not divorced from life. It is dialectic. It is ever changing and in revolt to the past. It has existed from the minds of free men for less than a century. Prior to this the direction of art was dictated by minds other than the artist for exploitation and commercial use. That the freedom of man's mind to celebrate his own feeling by a work of art parallels his social revolt from bondage. I believe that art is yet to be born and that freedom and equality are yet to be born.

If you ask me why I make sculpture, I must answer that it is my way of life, my balance, and my justification for being.

If you ask me for whom do I make art, I will say that it is for all who approach it without prejudice. My world, the objects I see are the same for all men of good will. The race for survival I share with all men who work for existence.

Yes, masterpieces are made today. Masterpieces are only works of art that people especially like. The twentieth century has produced very many. Present day contemporary America is producing masterpieces—a virile, aggressive, increasing number of painters and sculptors not before produced here. Let us not be intimidated by the pretending authorities who write books and term only this or that Mona Lisa as the only masterpiece. Masterpieces are only especially considered works of art. They occur now and they occurred 30,000 years ago.

Art is a paradox that has no laws to bind it. Laws set can always be violated. That confuses the pragmatic mind. There may exist conventionalized terminologies and common designations for periods, but no rules bind, either to the material substances from which it is made or the mental process of its concept. It is created by man's imagination in relation to his time. When art exists, it becomes tradition. When it is created, it represents a unity that did not exist before.

I feel no tradition. I feel great spaces.
I feel my own time. I am disconnected.
I belong to no mores—no party—no religion—
no school of thought—no institution.
I feel raw freedom and my own identity. I feel a
belligerence to museums, critics, art historians, aesthetes
and the so called cultural forces in a commercial order.

Zig VII, steel painted, 7/22/63

In this century and our country, the creative position has changed for both the painter and sculptor, in less than a decade. Artists have won battles of independence, and become fortified by great numbers, that they no longer feel the need to be loved. Their opinion, without organization or method, eventually determines art taste. Its avant garde rediscovers merit and elevates its own preferences before the connoisseurs are aware. The public knows nothing about it, until the connoisseur popularizes it. The professional connoisseurs can launch their choices but if it is not accepted by the artists, the elevation of a favorite does not stick. There are even critics in the artists' camp. A few museum officials grudgingly admit the avant garde force, but conduct themselves in the old order of slight condescension towards the artist. Contemporary collectors weigh more from a poll of the artists than from the opinions of connoisseurs. It is natural that artists know more about art than non artists. It is their total identity, they live it and make it.

The artist has a natural distrust of the museum, which is natural since their policies and positions are opposite.

Fine art is that produced by the mind of the creator.
   Other art produced to meet the minds and needs and needs of other people is commercial art.

The history of art, as it is called, does nothing for the creator.

The artist is working out a personal problem. It is doubtful that religion is any artist's problem.

The artist must work towards that which he does not know. Whether this is called invention or finding or searching, it must be a projection beyond the given state of art.

In the actual sense we should not stretch to invent but we should feel what has gone before us, and know what has been found; and what has been found is heritage, and what are problems are the things we are to find, the seeing of things from our vantage point, which is a place no artist has stood before, and not that of invention in the narrow sense but passionately found visions, because they are inspired answers to the problems of who we are in the time we are placed to speak.

Good sculpture is not decorative or designed to fill the space where once the architect appliqued his own scrolls of fauna form.

On rare occasions when the sculptor is called in by the architect, it appears to be an afterthought presenting a problem somewhat analogous to the making of a work of art to integrate for the modern motor car the place where the radiator cap used to be.

The painters have worked in mural size since Courbet. For a hundred years since impressionism, the architects have passed up works of art that were all within their large scale. From Monet and Rodin, Bonnard, Matisse, Picasso, Brancusi, Gargallo, Laurens and Lipchitz, Lachaise to 100 contemporary painters and a dozen sculptors, their full scale works have gone unsung by the architects.

In passing up the art of our century, the architect has generally commissioned artless anecdote. Rarely has art been used, and upon occasion, the architect has designed his own substitute.

As dwelling space contracts the size and concept of sculpture increases; I foresee no particular use other than aesthetic in society, least of all for architecture.

Sculpture has changed as an accessory to architecture—that has been its liberation—and that has put its costs directly upon the sculptor and made him pay for his freedom.

Mostly architects look down upon us and mostly architects are big business men here, and we're just one of their small clients in the building. They choose to put the marble in the men's room and they put the bronze in the fixtures and they really don't need sculptors at all.

I have no natural affinity to modern architecture. I can't afford to live in any of these buildings. It's not part of my world. My sculpture is part of my world; it's part of my everyday living; it reflects my studio, my house, my trees, the nature of the world I live in. And the nature of the world that painters and sculptors live in is a walkup, places with cracks; you look out the window and see chimney tops, and I don't think any of us can make the old fashioned royal bow to suit their needs. Liberty, or freedom of our position, is the greatest thing we've got.

Cubi II, stainless steel, 1962

Garage floor, Bolton Landing, *c.* 1960

I make no effort to generalize dispassionately. My statements are colored and prejudiced by my own concepts and experiences—and I cannot, like professional critics, lay down rules for a text. What are conviction aesthetics for me may not be for you. I believe in a firm union of all artists—with respect for each man's intellectual concept as in his choice of love.

In childhood we have been raped by word pictures. We must revolt against all word authority. Our only language is vision.

The division point between the artist and most writers of books on art history, museums and critics is the artist's belief that the present is the most important for making works of art. And that he is part of that present. To have other than that working belief would be to admit defeat.

The authorities are safer on past ground.

The creative process, the aesthetic also, natural and free in all of us in early life, becomes inhibited by externals, must be learned again. The understanding of art and the creative process is a battle against constant and powerful opposition.

Art is not didactic. It is not final. It is always waiting for projection by the viewer. From the creator's position the work represents a particular stage in his life based on the time, environment, art of the past, the history of his own works and even the shows, the dependent continuity of works to follow. In this particular sense a work of art is never finished. But in another sense, projection by the one perceiving it can bring it to completion.

I have spoken against tradition, but only the tradition of others who would hold art from moving forward. Tradition holding us to the perfection of others. In this context tradition can only say what art was, not what art is. Tradition comes wrapped up in word pictures, these are traps which lead laymen into cliché thinking. This leads to analogy and comparative evaluation and conclusion, especially in the hands of historians. Where conclusions are felt, the understanding of art has been hampered, and the innovations of the contemporary scene are often damned.

Art has its tradition, but it is a visual heritage. The artist's language is the memory from sight. Art is made from dreams and visions and things not known and least of all from things that can be said. It comes from the inside of who you are, when you face yourself. It is an inner declaration of purpose.

It is not the artist who talks the truth beauty stuff—and whenever it has been, it is his expression of other influences, a defensive and not an innate natural thing that the work is involved with.
the beauty of the act—in making—to be the truth

Real beauty in life is well fed girls in the house, black night, totally quiet except for symphony from WQXR—cleaned up shop—acid etching name and date on last finished work, new one going on the floor, and finished work about, sometimes the consciousness and the sequence bring the greatest glory I get . . .

Group: *Voltri XVIII; Voltri V;* both steel, 6/62

Cézanne 1839—1906

At the time Cézanne was painting—integrated, settled, calm, sure where he belonged—having relatives and tradition around him—my own family were felling trees for their own houses—clearing and breaking new soil, worrying about Indian raiders and the necessities of survival, the uncertainty of the new territory as a home establishment.

For what has gone before is my tradition.

There is nothing in art that there wasn't some of before.

To people whose reactions and response are conditioned by television, Hollywood, radio digests, the biased press, etc. I cannot hope to speak.

Voltri XX, steel, 6/62

The stingy logic of the philosopher, his suspicion that the irrational creative menaces the will, excludes all-important element of art making which I call affection. This feeling of affection which dominates art making has nothing to do with the philosopher's need for rationalization.

We must speak of affection—intense affection which the artist has for his work—an affection of relief, proudness, belligerent vitality, satisfaction and conviction. Can or do the critics, the audience, the philosophers ever possess the intensity of affection for the work which the creator possessed? Do they have the belligerent vitality of understanding which seems the attribute of contemporary work? Can they project this intense affection to the work of art?

We have all let anthropologists, philosophers, historians, connoisseurs and mercenaries, and everybody else tell us what art is or what it should be. But I think we ought to very simply let it be what the artist says it is. And what the artist says it is, you can see by his work. I would like to leave it just like that.

Voltri-Bolton VII, steel, 12/19/62

Voltron XXV, steel, 3/23/63

Voltri-Bolton I, steel, 12/6/62

Voltron XII, steel, 1/2/63

POEMS AND DREAMS

How little I know—until I see what happened in the night on
the snow—the movement of animals, their paths, and why—the animals
that fly the night birds leave no tracks except on the mind
the star tracks that angle to the earth sharp and direct
the broad brushing of the wind shown only by the snow plops
from branches—circuling the bushes and trees.

Voltron XVIII, steel painted, 1/29/63 (in foreground)

The Question—what are your influences—

From the history of art and the myth of woman
from the half of a part chewed chicken rib cage
and out of a fried salted mackerel spine
the structure of August hatched moths that come off the mountains
the color of moths that blind in my arc
out of Beethoven's E flat major, opus 31 and
the statement about intent he made at the time
from brush marks on a wall
the personages that grain pine boards
the grease spots on paper
the creatures in foliage
the statements of nature—the underlying structure
which forms the object, its whole or its parts—
related by associations not yet befouled by commerce
the nature of accident made by man as they fall in unity
as if directed by genes and generations
From Lahey's thrust, from Sloan's cones and cubes
from Matulka's cubist concept and aggressive inquiry
from Graham's eratic finesse from Davis' conversations
over ale at McSorleys or Stewarts over coffee, his
caustic disdain for the stuffed shirts in our professional
world, his enthusiasm for pine top Smith
From all my friends and contemporaries
Directives too come from the way swallows dart
The way trees fall
the shape of rocks
the color of a dry doe in brown
the way bark grows on basswood sprouts
the head of a turtle—the vertebrae
the memory of the soup it made
and the 52 ping pong balls it never laid
the roll of the mountains after the day's work
on the walk from the shop to my house
the way stars track
from bugs and butterflies under magnification
dividing to find the common denominators
the antennae, body movement to shape, the joints of the legs
and feet, squared by the memory of fish and the behavior of man
the ecstacy of a piano sonata and black coffee at midnight
the pieces finished outside the shop
the piece underway—the piece finished conceptually
the odds on the wall, the patterns in the rafters,
the stack of materials, the tools to form it and the work to come
the memory of 1 Atlantic Avenue, the odds on the wall,
the ship's ventilators that hung from the rafters, the
rusty rows of forging tongs
the banks of hardies, the forging beds, the babbit ladles
the stacks of buffalo horn
the boxes of barrier reef pearl shell
the baskets of pistol handles in various stages of finish and polish

146

the rows of every revolver frame ever made, the clatter of
barge fuel pumps, the backwater roll of an incoming ferry
the crunch of Levy the barge oiler walking thru the cinder
yard out the gate for coffee
from the way booms sling
from the ropes and pegs of tent tabernacles
and side shows at country fairs in Ohio
from the bare footed memory of unit relationships on
locomotives sidling thru Indiana,
from hopping freights, from putting the engines together and
working on their parts in Schenectady
From everything that happens to circles
and from the cultured forms of woman and the free growth
of mountain flowers . . .
From no one, individually, but selections
from the cube root of all in varying
context.

148

The Question—what is your hope

I would like to make sculpture that would rise from
water and tower in the air—
that carried conviction and vision that had not
existed before
that rose from a natural pool of clear water
to sandy shores with rocks and plants
that men could view as natural without reverence or awe
but to whom such things were natural because they were
statements of peaceful pursuit—and joined in the
phenomenon of life
Emerging from unpolluted water at which men could bathe
and animals drink—that
harboured fish and clams and all things natural to it
I dont want to repeat the accepted fact,
moralize or praise the past or sell a product
I want sculpture to show the wonder of man, that flowing water,
rocks, clouds, vegetation, have for the man in peace who
glories in existence
this sculpture will not be the mystical abode
of power of wealth of religion
Its existence will be its statement
It will not be a scorned ornament on a money changer's temple
or a house of fear
It will not be a tower of elevators and plumbing with every
room rented, deductions, taxes, allowing for depreciation
amortization yielding a percentage in dividends
It will say that in peace we have time
that a man has vision, has been fed, has worked
it will not incite greed or war
That hands and minds and tools and material made a symbol
to the elevation of vision
It will not be a pyramid to hide a royal corpse from pillage
It has no roof to be supported by burdened maidens
It has no bells to beat the heads of sinners
or clap the traps of hypocrites, no benediction
falls from its lights, no fears from its shadow
this vision cannot be of a single mind— a single concept,
it is a small tooth in the gear of man,
it was the wish incision in a cave,
the devotion of a stone hewer at Memphis
the hope of a Congo hunter
It may be a sculpture to hold in the hand
that will not seek to outdo by bulky grandeur
which to each man, one at a time, offers a marvel of
close communion, a symbol which answers to the holder's vision,
correlates the forms of woman and nature, stimulates the
recall sense of pleasurable emotion, that momentarily
rewards for the battle of being

Cubi VII, stainless steel, 3/28/63; with Rebecca and Candida Smith

Menand III, steel painted, 9/13/63

The Cloud

The floating body with the
Chimeric head of
a bird and a star for a
belly button—
The legs float out into
the tails of a nightshirt
all the fold pieces are
individual entities
with their own attributes
unrelated to clouds but
related to pebbles
on a beach—gallstones in a
bladder—curd in a
sour mash—soft like
begonia petals gently
moving to be drawn to
sugared taffy
The eye moon floats out
of the night trap the
star moves to kneecap.
The bird head turns to pickerel
the nightshirt rolls and falls
The nude body of begonia
scales trails milky spawn
The moon has moved to
the eye of a snarling tiger
and I wonder how many
of my Chinese friends are killed tonight

A structure that can face the sun
and hold its own
against the blaze and power, the heat of
its lemons and its eggs

Cubi I, stainless steel, 3/4/63

There is something rather noble about junk—selected junk—
junk which has in one era performed nobly in function for
common man—
has by function been formed by the smithy's hand alone
and without bearings roll or bell
has fulfilled its function, stayed behind,
is not yet relic or antique or precious
which has been seen by the eyes of all men and left for me—
to be found as the cracks in sidewalks
as the grain in wood
as the drops in grass
out of a snow hummock
as the dent in mud from
a bucket of poured storms
as the clouds float and
as beauties come
to be used, for an order
to be arranged
to be now perceived
by new ownership

The flight path of birds, moths insects
on a paper, songs in a high wind
the letters left behind on burnt paper
what left snow behind—the depth by wind and
the shade of trees—or man made shelter dip of land
who threw boards on a man planted
pile thus
is the truth of sounds
the distance of many miles
or what the eye sees at a hundred paces
or the size of a hummock big enough to stamp on
or the pile made by two hard fists
or a fresh baked oatmeal cookie
or is it who sees it . . .

the post with
limbs nailed to the
four sides upon
which mason jars
were hung to sun
dry, the glass jar
trees of Indiana
backyards

Highway 60 Illinois
A weathered hawk setting in a tree
feeling old and slow
feathers gone from the wing
one broken in the tail
watching the 70 mile traffic roar below
through fields of cotton brush and corn stubble

2 Circles 2 Crows, steel painted, 12/17/63;
in background: *Cubi VI*, stainless steel, 1963

Notes

watch a torn sheet of tissue paper roll over
and form in shifting winds
a basswood sprout—the green undercoat
grows so fast it breaks the brown outer layer—
force—energy—of growing things—

white birch

it writes a musical score before it dies

No shading so delicate as the gradations of muck and loam
chiaroscuro never showed greater contrast or more subtle identity
the roads of man in square mile bites—the greed of a walk
the sorrow of winter loneliness—and mud week (spring)
laid in squares—no 2 alike
hundreds of squares—and squared tilling
and then one dares to plow circles

Sketch of grass tufts in snow, ink, dated 1/19/1951

in Smith's handwriting:
"what happens to barnyard grass
when it emerges from snow
and takes on the characteristics
of the cows, the horse, the manure falls which nurture it

on a warm January 19, 1951 day, hay tufts
emerge from snow cover possessing all the
vertical and bent structure natural and the
envisioned lines of all female positions known—all the
thrusts of lines, all the curvature of forms"

The Landscape

I have never looked at a landscape without seeing
other landscapes
I have never seen a landscape without visions
of things I desire and despise
lower landscapes have crusts of heat—raw epidermis
and the choke of vines
the separate lines of salt errors—the monadnocks
of fungus
the balance of stone—with gestures to grow
the lost posts of manmade boundaries—in moulten
shade a petrified paperhanger who shot the duck
a landscape is a still life of Chaldean history
it has faces I do not know
its mountains are always sobbing females
it is bags of melons and prickle pears
its woods are sawed to boards
its black hills bristle with maiden fern
its stones are Assyrian fragments
it flows the bogside beauty of the river Liffey
it is colored by Indiana gas green
it is steeped in veritable indian yellow
it is the place I've traveled to and never found
it is somehow veiled to vision by pious bastards
and the lord of Varu the nobleman from Gascogne
in the distance it seems threatened by the destruction
of gold

The position for vision has undergone changes
The canvas is a flat—a mile or two up—
earth surface depth doesn't seem important—the importance
becomes pattern—
the importance of nature pattern in relation to man made pattern
from boundaries made by early work—relationship of work to area—
the roadways the drainage—the untillable—
How big a bite can a man take, can he manage more with machine—
change areas lines overlaid—yet from the upper view the old lines of
80 years ago still show—under soft snow the delicate lines of erosion—
the force of wind and solidifying action in use
the overlap—the dark openwater—the trapped snow—arrowheads—
the hairy figures of moraine
the crew cut woodlands
the once used form and force so soft and subtle
at a distance oil storage tanks and their moats
the 64 belly buttons for a hundred square miles

A dream is a dream never lost
I've had it inside a 4-8-4 on the top of a Diesel Engine,
they have been in a size dream.
I found an old flatcar
asked for, and was given it—

Had I used the flatcar for the base
and made a sculpture on the top
the dream would have been closer

I could have loaded a flatcar with
vertical sheets, inclined planes, uprights—
with holes, horizontals supported—

I could have made a car with
the nude bodies of machines,
undressed of their details and teeth—

I could have made a flatcar with
a hundred anvils of varying sizes and character
which I found at forge stations.

I could have made a flatcar with
painted skeletal wooden patterns

In a year I could have made a train

the flatcar I had is now melted

Wagon II, forged iron, 4/16/64

Group: *Cubi III*, stainless steel, 1962;
Cubi IX, stainless steel, 12/26/61

Cubi XXI, stainless steel, 1964

THE ARTIST'S IDENTITY

Beneath the whole art concept, every pass in the act,
every stroke, should be our own identity.

Wagon III, forged iron, 1964

I haven't named this work nor thought where it would go.
I haven't thought what it is for, except that it is made to be seen.
I've made it because it comes closer to who I am than any other
method I can use. The work is my identity.
There were no words in my mind during its creation and I'm certain
words are not needed in its seeing. And why should you expect
understanding when I do not? That is the marvel, to question but not
to understand. Seeing is the true language of perception. Understanding is for words. As far as I am concerned, after I've made the
work, I've said everything I can say.

I do not work with a conscious and specific conviction about a piece of sculpture.
It is always open to change and new association. It should be a celebration,
one of surprise, not one rehearsed. The sculpture work is a statement of my
identity. It is part of my work stream, related to my past works, the 3 or 4 in
process, and the work yet to come. In a sense it is never finished. Only the
essence is stated, the key presented to the beholder for further travel.

Untitled, stainless steel, 2/26/65

Identity can never be two things. It has one master. The practical question of survival while holding this identity I have not yet solved. But I do know that if I am forced to teach or work in a factory for survival, I am the artist who labors temporarily. The identity does not yield. I am never the teacher or factory worker who makes art.

I sat near my window and watched a workman trudge Hill Street, a workman with a striped bill cap overalls lunchpail carrying his coat, I looked at this man, I have seen this man when war makes it just a few years ago, twenty years from now I may be that man. Communism or fascism puts the artist if he survives into practical use. This is the creative artist's position in either of these societies.

I mention this because it relates to your identity. The most important thing to know is who you are and what you stand for, and to acknowledge this identity in your time. You can not go back. Art can not go back. The concepts in art are your history, there you start. The projection beyond your filial heritage is as vast as the past. The field for ideas is open and great, your heritage is universal, your position is equal to any in the world, except I can tell you no way to make a living at art.

Always remember that you are the artist, the creator, it is your own ego that is being satisfied. It is rewarding if others understand your aim, but it is never your duty to explain it. Honest rationalizing of just one work might take years—a complete psychoanalysis of the artist's life, an historical analysis of his art, (viz. the history of man), his physical condition, his knowledge of techniques and influences directed by his materials, all his fears, his visions. Assuredly no man's conscious mind retains it all. The result might be a twenty volume case history of just this one picture—and it is doubtful whether this case history would help in understanding the art. The picture was made for visual reception. So, if you the artist, if you are an inspired mind, if you feel that you can express something that has not been expressed before, if you are willing to lay yourself open to opprobrium and tough sledding in a wealthy country with a narrow culture—to be an artist—have the courage of conviction—for you will never be happy being anything else.

It is identity, and not that overrated quality called ability, which determines the artist's finished work. Ability is but one of the attributes and acts only in degree. Ability may produce a work but identity produces the works before and after. Ability may make the successful work in the eyes of the connoisseur, but identity can make the failures which are the most important to the artist. What the critics term the failures are apt to be unresolved but of greatest projection. They had to be done, they held the promise. The promise, the hint of new vista, the unresolved, the misty dream, the artist should love even more than the resolved, for here is the fluid force, the promise
and the search.

I like to eat
I like to see people eat
I don't like the presence of women to eat (in restaurants)
They pick
The portions are smaller
the attitude is less lusty
Of any place out that I like Locke-Ober's men's bar at noon best
The single men diners who sit on wing stools in front of
the weighted salavar covers, get fast service and really
eat—intent upon that—
When hungry it is a man's experience.
Of course the cigars are bad because of hypocrisy—
Kennedy smoked Havanas—so does Johnson—I see names in Dunhills

---

I can or have eaten 25c meat loaf with free salad and rolls—
with gin and a small beer chaser for 10c
I've made my work that way too—no less—always before love or food
(now not before daughters)

. . .

but
today Nov. 30 in Locke-Ober's
on a swinging stool
it's lobster bisque
baked oysters
winter place
bay scallops
and bacon
to hell with greens
and you stick the ¼ lemon under the hot pan to give odor
black bread with frosty edges
sweet butter
Things I don't get in the mountains.

We do not imitate nature

We are not the mirror of the external world
that is the camera

We are not even the illusionistic mirror

We are not the sweetness or light mirror

We are not the mirror of art historians

or art critics
or art philosophers

nor the collectors to glorify their own taste
or the museums to complete the chronology of their collections
if we mirror at all it is our own personal vision

with a statement that the artist is unique and individual—
dedicated and growing; and this work reflecting his creative power
is the best of his vision—but with the promise and always the promise

The insecurity of other things has forced work so much so that work is now a catharsis—and my only security.

The conscious things like cooking, cleaning, must be done with music or hastily done because work interruption was in a state of challenge and its return is anticipated and awaits a certain battle I must win or culminate.

Yet lonesomeness is a state in which the creative artist must dwell much of the time. The truly creative artist is projecting towards what he has not seen, and can only take the company of his identity. The adventure is alone and the process itself becomes actuality. It is him and the work. He has left the subject behind.

Becca, stainless steel, 4/30/65

And so this being the happiest—is disappointing, the heights come seldom—the steadiness is always chewing the gut—seldom without a raw spot—the times of true height are so rare some seemingly high spots being suspected later as illusion—such being those contacts with people wherein elation comes related to or in dependence with others—the worth of existence is doubtful but if stuck with it—seems no other way but to proceed—the future—the factory or the classroom both undesirable yet possible at present but in 20 years neither will be open—and, my cause may be no better—can I change my pursuit—not, and have even this much all of which I should be happy with—and nothing has been as great or as wonderful as I envisioned. I have confidence in my ability to create beyond what I have done, and always at the time beyond what I do—in what do I lack balance—ability to live with another person—that ability to have acquaintances—and no friends—what degrees make the difference—or am I unable to give what it takes—apparently I don't know what it is or is it illusion in middle minds—it would be nice to not be so lonesome sometimes—months pass without even the acquaintance of a mind. Acquaintances are pure waste—why do I measure my life by works—the other time seems waste—can the measured life by work be illusion—yet this standard seems farthest from illusion of any measure—and the way it stands much is lacking—and a certain body time tells that it can't be had, if it didn't come by now and so much work yet to be done—it comes too fast to get it down in solids—too little time too little money—why can't it stay as vision—for who else do I make it? The tensions from piling obligations—the goddamned ringing in my ears—the fucking lonesomeness —which is not only physical but mental—where did I miss in growing or is everybody else that way and lying to themselves with illusions—and that's no help to me the hole in my gut gnaws—I can live till May, yet what impends—why do I have to shit when I know it would only be guts—if I walk 15 miles through the mountains looking for Finnegan[1] I'm exhausted enough to want to rest and the mind won't—enjoying nature is only occasional and not complete enough—but more so than artificial stimulations of jazz and bop and beer which race along without the mind and leave me feeling cheated—I hate to go to bed—to stay alive longer—I've slipped up on time—it all didn't get in—the warpage is in me—I convey it to the person I live with—where do I find it to change—do I like it that way, am I glad it's too late—some yes some no—would financial security help—or why cannot part security till May be some appeasement.

Cubi XXVIII (Gate III), stainless steel, 1965

The trouble is, every time I make one sculpture, it breeds ten more, and the time is too short to make them all.

You know who I am and what I stand for. I have no allegiance, but I stand, and I know what the challenge is, and I challenge every-thing and everybody. And I think that is what every artist has to do. The minute you show a work, you challenge every other artist. And you have to work very hard, especially here. We don't have the introduction that European artists have. We're challenging the world . . . I'm going to work to the best of my ability to the day I die, challenging what's given to me.

Cubi XXVI, stainless steel, 1965

NOTES TO THE TEXT

David Smith's text and his note-book material are identified here either by the reel and frame number of the microfilm, hereafter referred to as R and F, in the Archives of American Art and/or by the note-book numbers and dates allocated to them by the Archives. Text used which did not originate in the Archives is so identified. Because Smith habitually repeated his texts in different speeches, with varying amounts of alterations, the references given here are generally only to the first appearance of such texts in the Archives. The reader can identify Smith's text by referring to the page in this book on which text appears; when more than one excerpt of text occurs on a page, the order of identification starts at the top of the column at the left.

FOREWORD

1. *Art in America*, No. One, 1966.
2. "David Smith" by Robert Motherwell, *Vogue*, February 1, 1965.
3. "For David Smith" by Robert Motherwell, Willard Gallery catalogue, April 1950.
4. From a letter to the editor
5. "The Sculpture of David Smith" by Hilton Kramer, *Arts*, February 1960.
6. *The New York Herald Tribune*, February 21, 1960.
7. *Art in America*, op. cit.
8. *Ibid.*
9. *Ibid.*
10. *Ibid.*

DAVID SMITH BY DAVID SMITH
Page 17 R 4 F 0360 (1952).

EVENTS IN A LIFE
Page 22 R 4 F 0751; 0490-9; Notebook 40 (1950–54).
24–33 R 4 F 0264–82.

1. Married Dorothy Dehner December 24, 1927.
2. Dorothy Dehner: "David drove a taxi for about two weeks. He would drive from 8 or 9 AM to dinner time; he used to come home for lunch. At that time we lived in a comparatively fancy neighborhood, and he didn't want anyone to know he drove a taxi, so he would park it a few blocks away and walk home. He wore an Alpine hat with a brush instead of a cap. One day he was threatened with an iron pipe by some other drivers because he parked in the wrong taxi stand area. Soon after that he stopped driving a taxi."
3. Dorothy Dehner: "We made small posters together for Birch Elixir for the people in the Rudolph Steiner cult."
4. Dorothy Dehner: "His job at Spalding was from February to May, before he went on the oil tanker. After the trip he returned to Spalding and continued work there until we went to the Virgin Islands."
5. Dorothy Dehner: "Matulka was the great influence on David's painting; but John Graham was a perfectly tremendous influence on his life and philosophic attitude. He introduced David to a wider world."
6. Visited the Virgin Islands from October 1931 to June 1932.
7. Dorothy Dehner: "David's first piece of sculpture was made from a piece of coral he found; it was a torso. His second piece was a Negro head which he painted brown—his first painted sculpture."
8. *Cahiers d'Art*, a then current French art publication.

9. Dorothy Dehner: "David learned much about cubism from John Graham, whom we met in 1929. We met Graham through the Furlongs (Thomas Furlong, painter, and his wife, Weber, Secretary of The Art Students' League) with whom we stayed as paying guests in Bolton."
10. Dorothy Dehner: "We had a 3-room apartment; David's studio was the only big room in the apartment. I used to follow him around with a sprinkling can to sprinkle water on the things that were catching fire."
11. Found studio at Terminal Iron Works, 1 Atlantic Ave., Brooklyn in spring of 1932.
12. Dorothy Dehner: "We always had rent money, we always had food, we had a car and a house in the country. Outside of necessities our money went mostly for his work. We never had a fight about money. He was anxious about money but that was another question."
13. First exhibited work at ACA Gallery in 1932.
14. Probably did not exhibit at Ferargil Gallery until 1934.
15. After David Smith's death, his executors found a letter written to him by Dorothy Dehner for his birthday in 1947. Smith had written the date on it and placed it in his grandmother's Bible. It is quoted here in full:
   David . . . Today is your birthday . . . happy birthday David . . . creator . . . genius is the vulgar word . . . I watch you make and I watch you do . . . and I am filled with wonder . . . and pride . . . it is rare to watch that quality . . . so few have it . . . and I am privileged. Thank you David. With the creation of your work comes life to the world . . . a new mans new ideas . . . undefinable in the true sense . . . defined they turn into something less than they are. . . . you will always keep on working David . . . no exhortations of the patriots of ART are needed . . . my wish for the year for you . . . work good . . . be happy as you can.

   D

   PS. Well . . . no PS.

16. Dorothy Dehner: "His grandmother died in the 1920's; she left him a very small sum. We went to Europe on our own money. This was the kind of thing David didn't want people to know."
17. Dorothy Dehner: "Despite the strain of travel, we did have a very good time. David was often frustrated because materials and technical knowhow were lacking, making it difficult for him to work. He smashed the castings against blocks of marble that were in front of our house."
18. Dorothy Dehner: "We used to lug David's sculpture around on the subway."
19. Dorothy Dehner: "Edgar Levy, painter, was terribly important to David."
20. Dorothy Dehner: "I think Herman Shumlin bought it for $8.50."
21. Dorothy Dehner: "Capitalist Perfidy! Oh David, you are right on this page."
22. Dorothy Dehner: "At that time we were wildly political. We judged everything on the basis of whether people were reactionaries or progressives."
23. Painter and friend of the Smiths. He now lives in Croton-on-Hudson, N.Y.

24. Dorothy Dehner: "For a first exhibition it did, in fact, arouse a lot of critical opinion. For one thing, *Time* printed a photograph and an article . . ."
25. This statement attributed by Smith to E. A. Jewell, art critic of *The New York Times*, is misquoted by Smith.
26. Neumann-Willard Gallery exhibition was in March 1940.
27. Dorothy Dehner: "This piece was in dark blue enamel—a bright, dark blue—with some red brush marks. The Museum of Modern Art saw it and asked to exhibit it in their garden, which they did."
28. See Note 26.
29. Clement Greenberg review appeared in *The Nation*, January 23, 1943.
30. *Head* (1938) was purchased by the Museum of Modern Art in 1943; subsequently the Museum acquired other pieces.
31. Willard Gallery exhibit in 1940 was the show of *Medals for Dishonor* held in November.
32. In the British Museum he saw satirical medals made to be given to the Germans for their bombings; they gave him the first idea for his medals.
33. Dorothy Dehner: "He did work nights. He had enormous capacity for work. I've never known anybody who could undo his knots through work the way he did."
34. Marian Willard.
35. See note 31.
36. Dorothy Dehner: "It is true that at those levels David had a lot of appreciation. For example, Leroy Davidson, who now teaches art history at UCLA, looked at the medals and said, 'These are the greatest works in metal since the Renaissance.'"
37. Dorothy Dehner: "He means Dr. Milgram, an orthopedist not a pediatrician."
38. Dorothy Dehner: "The first part of this should read, 'check spelling of Milgram'; the second part refers to Elisofon, a photographer for *Life*."
39. Dorothy Dehner: "We called them caviar plates; they were just shells on which we used to put caviar because it looked so great on them."
40. Dorothy Dehner: "These were made in wax."
41. Dorothy Dehner: "I raised a terrific garden. I canned about 700 jars of stuff that year."
42. Dorothy Dehner: "David was 37 then, right near the age limit. When he was refused because of sinus trouble, we felt very happy and relieved; the army would have been impossible for him."
43. Dorothy Dehner: "The old house was a real shack. It was falling apart and was full of rats. All our savings went towards this new house, for we knew we would have to build it some day."
44. Dorothy Dehner: "Yes, I moved to New York City. I had to get away for a while. David was in a bad state. For one thing, some time before, he had an accident; he was knocked off the running board of a truck, it was a terrible thing. On top of this, he was going through the most awful inner turmoil and conflict. I stayed in New York 5 months; David joined me from January to April, and then we went back up to the farm and started plans for building our new house."

LIST OF SCULPTURE ILLUSTRATED

Page number is indicated in bold face.
(Titles are from left to right when groups are reproduced.)

LIST OF DRAWINGS ILLUSTRATED